MATTHEW

Chapters 1—13

J. Vernon McGee

THOMAS NELSON PUBLISHERS

Nashville • Atlanta • London • Vancouver

Published in Nashville, Tennessee, by Thomas Nelson, Inc.

Scripture quotations are from the KING JAMES VERSION of the Bible.

Library of Congress Cataloging-in-Publication Data

McGee, J. Vernon (John Vernon), 1904–1988
   [Thru the Bible with J. Vernon McGee]
   Thru the Bible commentary series / J. Vernon McGee.
      p.   cm.
   Reprint. Originally published: Thru the Bible with J. Vernon McGee. 1975.
   Includes bibliographical references.
   ISBN 0-7852-1037-7 (TR)
   ISBN 0-7852-1097-0 (NRM)
   1. Bible—Commentaries. I. Title.
BS491.2.M37   1991
220.7′7—dc20
                                    90–41340
                                        CIP

PRINTED IN MEXICO

20 - 07

CONTENTS

MATTHEW—Chapters 1—13

PREFACE

The radio broadcasts of the Thru the Bible Radio five-year program were transcribed, edited, and published first in single-volume paperbacks to accommodate the radio audience.

There has been a minimal amount of further editing for this publication. Therefore, these messages are not the word-for-word recording of the taped messages which went out over the air. The changes were necessary to accommodate a reading audience rather than a listening audience.

These are popular messages, prepared originally for a radio audience. They should not be considered a commentary on the entire Bible in any sense of that term. These messages are devoid of any attempt to present a theological or technical commentary on the Bible. Behind these messages is a great deal of research and study in order to interpret the Bible from a popular rather than from a scholarly (and too-often boring) viewpoint.

We have definitely and deliberately attempted "to put the cookies on the bottom shelf so that the kiddies could get them."

The fact that these messages have been translated into many languages for radio broadcasting and have been received with enthusiasm reveals the need for a simple teaching of the whole Bible for the masses of the world.

I am indebted to many people and to many sources for bringing this volume into existence. I should express my especial thanks to my secretary, Gertrude Cutler, who supervised the editorial work; to Dr. Elliott R. Cole, my associate, who handled all the detailed work with the publishers; and finally, to my wife Ruth for tenaciously encouraging me from the beginning to put my notes and messages into printed form.

Solomon wrote, ". . . of making many books there is no end; and much study is a weariness of the flesh" (Eccl. 12:12). On a sea of books that flood the marketplace, we launch this series of THRU THE BIBLE with the hope that it might draw many to the one Book, The Bible.

J. VERNON MCGEE

The Gospel According to

MATTHEW

INTRODUCTION

The Gospel of Matthew, although it is only twenty-eight chapters long, is a very important book. In fact, Genesis and Matthew are the two key books of the Bible.

As we come today to the Gospel of Matthew, I'd like to bridge the gap between the Old Testament and the New Testament because, in order to appreciate and to have a right understanding of the New Testament, it is almost essential to know something about this period of approximately four hundred years. This is the time span between the days of Nehemiah and Malachi and the birth of Jesus Christ in Bethlehem. You see, after Malachi had spoken, heaven went silent. Station G O D went off the air, and there was no broadcasting for four hundred years. Then one day the angel of the Lord broke in upon the time of prayer when there was a priest by the name of Zacharias standing at the altar in Jerusalem. The angel gave the announcement of the birth of John the Baptist who was the forerunner of the Lord Jesus. We shall see later how important John the Baptist is in the Gospel of Matthew.

We find that a great deal took place in this interval of four hundred years even though it is a silent period as far as Scripture is concerned. This period was a thrilling and exciting time in the history of these people, and in many ways it was also a tragic time. The internal condition of Judah experienced a radical transformation. A new culture, different institutions, and unfamiliar organizations arose in this period, and many of these new things appear in the New Testament.

World history had made tremendous strides in the interval between the Old and New Testaments. The Old Testament closed with the Medo-Persian Empire being the dominant power. Also, Egypt was still a power to be reckoned with in world politics. During the interval between the testaments, both faded from the scene as outstanding nations. World power shifted from the East to the West, from the Orient to the Occident, from Asia to Europe, and from Medo-Persia to Greece. When the New Testament opens, a new power, Rome, is the world ruler. A consideration of some important dates will give a bird's-eye view of this great transition period. (Because historians differ in their dating, consider these dates as approximate.)

480 B.C. Xerxes, the Persian, was victorious against the Greeks at Thermopylae but was defeated at the battle of Salamis. Actually, it was a storm that defeated him. This was the last bid of the East for world dominion.

333 B.C. Out of the West there came that "goat" which Daniel records in the eighth chapter of Daniel. This was Alexander the Great, the goat with the great horn. He led the united Greek forces to victory over the Persians at Issus.

332 B.C. Alexander the Great visited Jerusalem. He was shown the prophecy of Daniel which spoke of him; therefore he spared Jerusalem. Jerusalem was one of the few cities that he ever spared.

323 B.C. Alexander died way over in Persia. Apparently he had intended to move the seat of his empire there. Then the world empire of both East and West was divided among his four generals.

320 B.C. Judea was annexed to Egypt by Ptolemy Soter.

312 B.C. Seleucus founded the kingdom of the Seleucidae, which is Syria. He attempted to take Judea, and so Judea became the battleground between Syria and Egypt. This little country became a buffer state.

203 B.C. Antiochus the Great took Jerusalem, and Judea passed under the influence of Syria.

170 B.C. Antiochus Epiphanes took Jerusalem and defiled the temple. He had been mentioned in Daniel as the "little horn" (Dan. 8:9). He has been called the "Nero of Jewish history."

166 B.C. Mattathias, the priest of Judea, raised a revolt against Syria. This is the beginning of the Maccabean period. Probably the nation of Israel has never suffered more than during this era, and they were never more heroic than during this interval. Judas Maccabaeus, whose name means "the hammer," was the leader who organized the revolt.

63 B.C. Pompey, the Roman, took Jerusalem, and the people of Israel passed under the rulership of a new world power. They were under Roman government at the time of the birth of Jesus and throughout the period of the New Testament.

40 B.C. The Roman senate appointed Herod to be king of Judea. There never has been a family or a man more wicked than this. One can talk about the terrible Mafia, but this family would exceed them all.

37 B.C. Herod took Jerusalem and slew Antigonus, the last of the Maccabean king-priests.

31 B.C. Caesar Augustus became emperor of Rome.

19 B.C. The construction of the Herodian temple was begun. The building had been going on quite awhile when our Lord was born and was still continuing during the time of the New Testament.

4 B.C. Our Lord Jesus was born in Bethlehem.

Radical changes took place in the internal life of the nation of Judea because of their experiences during the intertestamental period. After the Babylonian captivity, they turned from idolatry to a frantic striving for legal holiness. The Law became an idol to them. The classic Hebrew gave way to the Aramaic in their everyday speech, although the Hebrew was retained for their synagogues. The synagogue seems to have come into existence after the captivity. It became the center of their life in Judea and everywhere else they went in the world. Also, there arose among these people a group of parties which are mentioned in the New Testament and are never even heard of in the Old Testament:

1. *PHARISEES*—The Pharisees were the dominant party. They

arose to defend the Jewish way of life against all foreign influences. They were strict legalists who believed in the Old Testament. They were nationalists in politics and wanted to restore the kingdom to the line of David. So they were a religo-political party. Today we would call them fundamental theologically and to the far right politically.

2. *SADDUCEES*—The Sadducees were made up of the wealthy and socially-minded who wanted to get rid of tradition. By the way, does that remind you of the present hour? Isn't it interesting that the rich families of this country are liberal? The crumbs still fall from the rich man's table. They are willing to give the crumbs, but they don't give their wealth, that is sure. The Sadducees were liberal in their theology, and they rejected the supernatural. Thus they were opposed to the Pharisees. The Sadducees were closely akin to the Greek Epicureans whose philosophy was "eat, drink, and be merry, for tomorrow we die." We may have a mistaken idea of the Sadducees. Actually, they were attempting to attain the "good life." They thought that they could overcome their bodily appetites by satisfying them, that by giving them unbridled reign, they would no longer need attention. In our day, a great many folk have this same philosophy. It did not work in the past; neither will it work today.

3. *SCRIBES*—The scribes were a group of professional expounders of the Law, stemming back from the days of Ezra. They became the hair-splitters. They were more concerned with the *letter* of the Law than with the *spirit* of the Law. When old Herod called in the scribes and asked where Jesus was to be born, they knew it was to be in Bethlehem. You would think that they would have hitchhiked a ride on the back of the camels to go down to Bethlehem to see Him, but they weren't interested. They were absorbed in the letter of the Law.

My friend, there is a danger of just wanting the information and the knowledge from the Bible but failing to translate it into shoe leather, not letting it become part of our lives. Through study we can learn the basic facts of Scripture, and all the theological truth contained in it, without allowing the Word of God to take possession of our hearts. The scribes fell into such a category. In our own day, I must confess that some of the most hardhearted people I meet are fundamentalists. They are willing to rip a person apart in order to maintain some little point. It is important to know the Word of God—that is a laudable attainment—but also we are to translate it into life and pass it on to others.

4. *HERODIANS*—The Herodians were a party in the days of Jesus, and they were strictly political opportunists. They sought to maintain the Herods on the throne, because they wanted their party in power.

The intertestamental period was a time of great literary activity in spite of the fact there was no revelation from God. The Old Testament was translated into Greek in Alexandria, Egypt, during the period from 285 to 247 B.C. It was translated by six members from each of the twelve tribes; hence, the name given to this translation was *Septuagint*, meaning "seventy." This translation was used by Paul, and our Lord apparently quoted from it.

The Apocrypha of the Old Testament was written in this era. These are fourteen books which bear no marks of inspiration. There are two books classified as the Pseudepigrapha, *Psalter of Solomon* and the *Book of Enoch*. They bear the names of two characters of the Old Testament, but there is no evidence that these two men were the writers.

Although this was a period marked by the silence of God, it is evident that God was preparing the world for the coming of Christ. The Jewish people, the Greek civilization, the Roman Empire, and the seething multitudes of the Orient were all being prepared for the coming of a Savior, insomuch that they produced the scene which Paul labeled, in Galatians 4:4, "the fulness of time." The four Gospels are directed to the four major groups in the world of that day.

The Gospel of Matthew was written to the nation Israel. It was first written in Hebrew, and it was directed primarily to the religious man of that time.

The Gospel of Mark was directed to the Roman. The Roman was a man of action who believed that government, law, and order could control the world. A great many people feel that is the way it should be done today. It is true that there must be law and order, but the Romans soon learned that they couldn't rule the world with that alone. The world needed to hear about One who believed in law and order but who also offered the forgiveness of sins and the grace and the mercy of God. This is the Lord whom the Gospel of Mark presents to the Romans.

The Gospel of Luke was written to the Greek, to the thinking man.

The Gospel of John was written directly for believers but indirectly for the Orient where there were the mysterious millions, all crying out in that day for a deliverance.

There is still a crying out today from a world that needs a Deliverer. The religious man needs Christ and not religion. The man of power needs a Savior who has the power to save him. The thinking man needs One who can meet all his mental and spiritual needs. And certainly the wretched man needs to know about a Savior who not only can save him but build him up so that he can live for God.

The Gospel of Matthew was written by a publican whom the Lord Jesus had put His hand upon in a very definite way (see Matt. 9:9). He was a follower, a disciple, of the Lord Jesus. Papias says, Eusebius confirms, and other of the apostolic fathers agree, that this Gospel was written originally by Matthew in Hebrew for the nation Israel, a religious people.

I don't have time to give the background of all this, but God has prepared this whole nation for the coming of Christ into the world. And He did come of this nation, as the Lord Jesus Himself said, ". . . salvation is of the Jews" (John 4:22). It was a great German historian who said that God prepared the Savior to come out of Israel— "salvation is of the Jews"—and He prepared the heathen for salvation, because they were lost and needed it.

This remarkable book is a key book of the Bible because it swings back into the Old Testament and gathers up more Old Testament prophecies than any other book. One might expect it to do this since it was first written to the Jews. But then, it moves farther into the New Testament than any of the other Gospels. For instance, no other Gospel writer mentions the church by name; but Matthew does. He is the one who relates the Word of our Lord, ". . . upon this rock I will build my church . . ." (Matt. 16:18). Even Renan, the French skeptic, said of this Gospel that it "is the most important book in Christendom, the most important that has ever been written." That is a remarkable statement coming from him! Matthew, a converted publican, was the choice of the Spirit of God to write this Gospel primarily to the people of Israel.

The Gospel of Matthew presents the program of God. The "Kingdom of Heaven" is an expression which is peculiar to this Gospel. It occurs thirty-two times. The word kingdom occurs fifty times. A proper understanding of the phrase "Kingdom of Heaven" is essential to any interpretation of this Gospel and of the Bible. May I make this statement right now, and I do make it categorically and dogmatically: The Kingdom and the church are not the same. They are not synonymous terms. Although the church is in the Kingdom, there is all the difference in the world.

For instance, Los Angeles is in California, but Los Angeles is not California. If you disagree, ask the people from San Francisco. California is not the United States, but it is in the United States. The Chamber of Commerce may think it is the United States, but it's not. It's only one-fiftieth of it.

Likewise, the church is in the Kingdom, but the Kingdom of Heaven, simply stated, is the reign of the heavens over the earth. The church is in this Kingdom. Now I know that theologians have really clouded the atmosphere, and they certainly have made this a very complicated thing. Poor preachers like I am must come up with a simple explanation, and this is it: the Kingdom of Heaven is the reign of the heavens over the earth. The Jews to whom this Gospel was directed understood the term to be the sum total of all the prophecies of the Old Testament concerning the coming of a King from heaven to set up a Kingdom on this earth with heaven's standard. This term was not new to them (see Dan. 2:44; 7:14, 27).

The Kingdom of Heaven is the theme of this Gospel. The One who is going to establish that Kingdom on the earth is the Lord Jesus. The Kingdom is all important. The Gospel of Matthew contains three major discourses concerning the Kingdom.

1. The Sermon on the Mount. That is the law of the Kingdom. I think it is only a partial list of what will be enforced in that day.

2. *The Mystery Parables.* These parables in Matthew 13 are about the Kingdom. Our Lord tells us that the Kingdom of Heaven is like a sower, like a mustard seed, and so on.

3. *The Olivet Discourse.* This looks forward to the establishment of the Kingdom here upon this earth.

It will be seen that the term "Kingdom of Heaven" is a progressive term in the Gospel of Matthew. This is very important for us to see. There is a movement in the Gospel of Matthew, and if we miss it, we've missed the Gospel. It is like missing a turn-off on the freeway. You miss it, brother, and you're in trouble. So if we miss the movement in this marvelous Gospel, we miss something very important.

This Gospel is very much like the Book of Genesis. They are two key books of the Bible, and you really should be familiar enough with these two books so that you can *think* your way through them. I will be giving you chapter headings so you can learn to think your way through the book. I would tell my students in former days, "When you can't sleep at night, don't count sheep. Instead, think your way through Genesis. Then think your way through the Gospel of Matthew. Take it up chapter by chapter. Chapter One: what is it about? Chapter Two: what is it about? If you say to me that you don't like counting sheep or chapters, then talk to the Shepherd, but the finest way to talk to the Shepherd is to go through these two books. That will help you to get acquainted with Him and come to know Him." By the way, it's more important to have Him talk to us than for us to talk to Him. I don't know that I've got too much to tell Him, but He has a lot to tell me. I suggest that you learn the chapters of Matthew so that you don't miss the movement in them.

Now I want to give you one way of dividing the Gospel of Matthew. I'll follow a little different division, but this will help you to think it through. It is important to know Matthew in order to understand the Bible!

1. **Person** of the King
    Chapters 1—2
2. **Preparation** of the King
    Chapters 2—4:16

OUTLINE

CHAPTERS

1 Genealogy and Record of Virgin Birth of Jesus

2 Visit of Wise Men—Flight to Egypt—Return to Nazareth

3 John the Baptist, Forerunner of King, Announces Kingdom and Baptizes Jesus, the King

4 Testing of the King in Wilderness—Begins Public Ministry at Capernaum—Calls Disciples

5—7 Sermon on the Mount
  (1) Relationship of Subjects of Kingdom to Self, 5:1–16
  (2) Relationship of Subjects of Kingdom to Law, 5:17–48
  (3) Relationship of Subjects of Kingdom to God, 6:1–34
  (4) Relationship of Children of King to Each Other, 7:1–29

8 Six Miracles of King Demonstrate His Dynamic to Enforce Ethics of Sermon on Mount

9 Performs Six More Miracles—Calls Matthew—Contends with Pharisees

10 Jesus Commissions Twelve to Preach Gospel of the Kingdom to Nation Israel

11 Quizzed by Disciples of John—Rejects Unrepentant Cities—Issues New Invitation to Individuals

12 Conflict and Final Break of Jesus with Religious Rulers

13 Mystery Parables of Kingdom of Heaven

CHAPTER 1

THEME: The genealogy of Jesus Christ and record of
the virgin birth of Jesus

THE GENEALOGY

The genealogy which opens the Gospel of Matthew and the New
Testament is in many respects the most important document in
the Scriptures. The entire Bible rests upon its accuracy. You will notice it has three divisions:
1. Genealogy from Abraham to David (vv. 1–6).
2. Genealogy from Solomon to the Babylonian captivity (vv. 7–
   11).
3. Genealogy from the Babylonian captivity to Joseph, the carpenter (vv. 12–17).
In our study of Genesis, we note the fact that it is a book about families. The genealogies there are very important, and we see them here
as we start the New Testament.

Now I must confess that at first this looks rather boring. You give
someone a New Testament, and they begin here in the Gospel of Matthew with a genealogy staring them in the face, and they're not going
to get very far in it. A chaplain friend of mine told me that in World
War II he gave out literally thousands of New Testaments to service-
men. He's seen the men in the bunks open the New Testament, read for
a minute or two at the beginning of Matthew, start through that genealogy and come to the conclusion this Book wasn't for them. Can't
blame them! My point is that we ought to use a little wisdom in giving
out literature to people. The average person should start first in any
one of the other three Gospels, preferably Mark, rather than the Gospel
of Matthew. But that doesn't lessen the importance of this genealogy.

The New Testament rests upon the accuracy of this genealogy because it establishes the fact that the Lord Jesus Christ is of the line of
Abraham and of the line of David. Both are very important. The line of

Abraham places Him in the nation, and the line of David puts Him on the throne—He is in that royal line.

The genealogies were very important to the nation Israel, and through them it could be established whether a person had a legitimate claim to a particular line. For example, when Israel returned from the captivity, we find in the Book of Ezra, "These sought their register among those that were reckoned by genealogy, but they were not found: therefore were they, as polluted, put from the priesthood" (Ezra 2:62). It was possible in Ezra's day to check the register of the tribe of Levi and remove those who made a false claim.

Evidently these genealogies were kept by the government and were accessible to the public. I have a notion they were kept in the temple because Israel was a theocracy, and actually the "church" and the state were one. This genealogy was obviously on display and could have been copied from the public records until the temple was destroyed in A.D. 70. The enemies of Jesus could have checked them and probably did. This is interesting and important because they challenged every move of the Lord Jesus, even offering a substitute explanation for the Resurrection, but they never did question His genealogy. The reason must be that they checked it out and found that it was accurate.

This is most important because it puts Jesus in a very unique position. You remember that He said the Shepherd of the sheep enters in by the door but the thief and the robber climb up some other way to get into the sheepfold (see John 10:1–2). That "fold" is the nation Israel. He didn't climb into the fold over a fence in the back, and He didn't come in through the alley way. He came in through the gate. He was born in the line of David and in the line of Abraham. This is what Matthew is putting before us. He is the fulfillment of everything that had been mentioned in the Old Testament. So the enemies of Christ never could challenge Him in regard to His genealogy. They had to find some other ways to challenge Him, and, of course, they did.

When I was a teenager, I became interested in the Bible for the first time, and I went to a summer conference where the Lord spoke to my heart. Our Bible teacher thrilled my heart as he taught the Word of God. One morning he asked, "How many of you young people have read the Bible through in a year?" There were two to three hundred young people there, but not a hand went up. He asked the same question four times. Finally, one young man in the back put up his hand rather hesitatingly and said, "Well, I read it, but I only read the parts that were interesting. I didn't read the genealogies." Everybody laughed, and the teacher laughed, too, and admitted that he didn't read them either. At that very moment it occurred to me that since the Spirit of God has used so much printer's ink to give them to us, there must be some importance in them for us. So I'll have you note this genealogy now in Matthew because it is very important.

This is the genealogy of the Lord Jesus on Joseph's side. We'll have another when we get over to Luke, and that will be from Mary's side.

The book of the generation of Jesus Christ, the son of David, the son of Abraham [Matt. 1:1].

"The book of the generation" is a phrase which is peculiar to Matthew. It's a unique expression, and you won't find it anywhere else in the New Testament. If you start going back through the Old Testament, back through Malachi and Zechariah and Haggai and back to the Pentateuch, through Deuteronomy, Numbers, Leviticus, Exodus into Genesis, you'll almost come to the conclusion that it's nowhere else in the Bible except here in Matthew. Then all of a sudden, you come to the fifth chapter of Genesis and see "This is the book of the generations of Adam . . ." (Gen. 5:1). There is that expression again. There are two books: the book of the generations of Adam and the book of the generation of Jesus Christ. How did you get into the family of Adam? You got in by a birth. You didn't perform it; in fact, you had nothing to do with it. But that's the way you and I got into the family of Adam. We got there by birth. But in Adam all die (Rom. 5:12). Adam's book is a book of death.

Then there is the other book, the book of the generation of Jesus Christ. How did you get into that family, into that genealogy? You got into it by a birth, the new birth. The Lord Jesus says we must be born again to see the Kingdom of God (see John 3:3). That puts us in the Lamb's Book of Life, and we get there by trusting Christ. We all are in the first book, the book of the generations of Adam. I trust that you, my friend, are also in the Lamb's Book of Life.

Matthew says Jesus is "the son of David, the son of Abraham." Didn't Matthew know that Abraham came before David? Of course he did because he makes that clear in the rest of the genealogy. Then why did he put it this way? He is presenting the Lord Jesus as the Messiah, the One who is the King, the One who is to establish the Kingdom of Heaven on earth. And that comes first. He must be in the line of David in fulfillment of the prophecies that God made to David. He is the Son of David.

He is also the Son of Abraham and it is very important that He be the Son of Abraham, because God had said to Abraham, ". . . in thy seed shall all the nations of the earth be blessed . . ." (Gen. 22:18). And in Galatians 3:16 Paul explains who that "seed" is: "Now to Abraham and his seed were the promises made. He saith not, And to seeds, as of many; but as of one, and to thy seed, which is Christ." So Jesus Christ is the Son of Abraham.

> **Abraham begat Isaac; and Isaac begat Jacob; and Jacob begat Judas and his brethren;**
>
> **And Judas begat Phares and Zara of Thamar; and Phares begat Esrom; and Esrom begat Aram;**
>
> **And Aram begat Aminadab; and Aminadab begat Naasson; and Naasson begat Salmon;**
>
> **And Salmon begat Booz of Rachab; and Booz begat Obed of Ruth; and Obed begat Jesse;**
>
> **And Jesse begat David the king; and David the king begat Solomon of her that had been the wife of Urias [Matt. 1:2–6].**

A careful look at the genealogy that follows is not only interesting; it is actually thrilling. Four names stand out as if they were in neon lights. It is startling to find them included in the genealogy of Christ.

First, they are the names of women; second, they are the names of Gentiles.

Customarily, the names of women did not appear in Hebrew genealogies, but don't find fault with that for the very simple reason that today we have the same thing in marriage. In a marriage the name that the couple takes is the name of the man. They don't take the name of the woman. Her line ends; his goes on. That's the way we do it today, and that's the way they did it then.

Down through the years I have performed marriages in which the girl had a lovely name like Jones or Smith, and she wanted to exchange it for a name like Neuenschwander or Schicklegruber! You would think that she'd not want to surrender her name for one having four or five syllables, but that's the way they do it today. I have a clipping in my file of about ten years ago that tells of a couple in Pasadena who did the unusual thing of taking the name of the woman, which, I understand, can be legally done. But our custom is to take the name of the man, and it is the man's genealogy that is given.

In Jesus' day it was indeed unusual to find in a genealogy a woman's name—yet here we have four names. They are not only four women; they are four Gentiles. As you know, God in the Law said that His people were not to intermarry with tribes that were heathen and pagan. Even Abraham was instructed by God to send back to his people to get a bride for his son Isaac. Also, the same thing was done by Isaac for his son Jacob. It was God's arrangement that monotheism should be the prevailing belief of those who were in the line that was leading down to the Lord Jesus Christ. Yet in His genealogy are the names of four gentile women—two of them were Canaanites, one was a Moabite, and the fourth was a Hittite! You would naturally ask the question, "How did they get into the genealogy of Christ?"

"Thamar" is the first one, and she is mentioned in verse three. Her story is in Genesis 38, and there she is called Tamar. That chapter is one of the worst in the Bible. Thamar got into the genealogy because she was a sinner.

"Rachab" is the next one mentioned in verse five. She's not a very pretty character in her story back in Joshua chapter 2 where she is called Rahab. But she did become a wonderful person after she came to a knowledge of the living and true God. "By faith the harlot Rahab perished not with them that believed not, when she had received the spies with peace" (Heb. 11:31). She got into the genealogy of Christ for the simple reason that she *believed*. She had faith. Notice the progression here. Come as a *sinner*, and then reach out the hand of *faith*.

"Ruth" is the next one mentioned in verse five. She is a lovely person, and you won't find anything wrong with her. But at Ruth's time there was the Law which shut her out because it said that a Moabite or an Ammonite shall not enter into the congregation of the Lord (see Deut. 23:3). Although the Law kept her out, there was a man by the name of Boaz who came into his field one day and saw her. It was love at first sight.

Now, maybe you didn't know that I believe in love at first sight. I proposed to my wife on our second date, and the only reason I didn't propose on our first date was because I didn't want her to think I was in a hurry! I do believe in love at first sight. But don't misunderstand me—we waited a year before we were married, just to make sure. And I think that is always the wise thing to do.

Boaz loved Ruth at first sight, and he extended grace to her by putting his mantle around her and bringing her, a Gentile, into the congregation of Israel. She asked, ". . . Why have I found grace in thine eyes . . . ?" (Ruth 2:10). You and I can ask that same question of God regarding His grace to us. Again, note the progression. We come as *sinners* and hold out the hand of *faith*, and He, by His marvelous grace, *saves* us.

"Bathsheba" is not mentioned by name but called "her that had been the wife of Urias" (v. 6). Her name isn't mentioned because it wasn't her sin. It was David's sin, and David was the one that really had to pay for it. And he did pay for it. She got into the genealogy of Christ because God does not throw overboard one of His children who sins. A sheep can get out of the fold and become a lost sheep, but we have a Shepherd who goes after sheep and always brings them back into the fold. He brought David back. So this is the whole story of salvation right here in this genealogy.

Now there are some more interesting things about this genealogy.

If you will compare this genealogy with the one in 1 Chronicles 3 (some of the names are spelled differently), you will find that in verse eight of Matthew, the names of Ahaziah, Joash, and Amaziah are left out. This shows that genealogies are quoted to give us a view of a certain line of descendants and that every individual is not necessarily named in every genealogy of the Bible. I think we should remember this in the genealogies given to us in Genesis before the Flood. These are not necessarily complete genealogies, but they are given to trace a certain line for us. I personally think man has been on this earth a lot longer than Ussher's dating which is found in the margins of many editions of the Bible. Remember that these dates are by *Ussher* and are not part of the Bible. They are faulty and do not belong there.

> **And Ezekias begat Manasses; and Manasses begat Amon; and Amon begat Josias;**
>
> **And Josias begat Jechonias and his brethren, about the time they were carried away to Babylon [Matt. 1:10–11].**

In verse 11, we find that Matthew skips Jehoiakim but includes Jechonias. Jechonias deserves our special attention because God had said that none of his seed would sit on the throne. "As I live, saith the LORD, though Coniah [his name is Jeconiah, but God took the Je off his name because it is the prefix for *Jehovah*, and this man was a wicked king] the son of Jehoiakim king of Judah were the signet upon my right hand, yet would I pluck thee thence. . . . Thus saith the LORD, Write ye this man childless, a man that shall not prosper in his days: for no man of his seed shall prosper, sitting upon the throne of David, and ruling any more in Judah" (Jer. 22:24, 30). Because of the sin of this man Jechonias, no one in his line could ever sit on the throne of David. You see, Joseph is in this line, but Joseph is not the natural father of Jesus. This is one of the most remarkable facts in the Scriptures, and Matthew is trying to make it clear to us. Joseph gave to Jesus the title, the *legal* title, to the throne of David because Joseph was the husband of Mary who was the one who bore Jesus. Jesus Christ is not

the seed of Joseph, nor is He the seed of Jeconiah. But both Joseph and
Mary had to be from the line of David, and they were—through two
different lines from two different sons of David. We'll find when we
get to Luke that Mary's line comes from David through his son Na-
than. Joseph's line comes through the royal line through Solomon. So
Joseph and Mary both had to go to Bethlehem to be enrolled for taxa-
tion because they were both from the line of David. You see how interesting, fascinating, and important these genealogies are and how
much they are worth our study.

Now the genealogy concludes with this verse—

**And Jacob begat Joseph the husband of Mary, of whom
was born Jesus, who is called Christ [Matt. 1:16].**

You see that this breaks the pattern which began as far back as verse 2
where it says that Abraham *begat* Isaac. From then on it was just a
whole lot of "begetting," and verse 16 begins by saying, "And Jacob
begat Joseph." You would expect it to continue by saying that Joseph
begat Jesus, but it does not say that. Instead, it says, "Jacob begat Joseph the husband of Mary, of whom was born Jesus, who is called
Christ." Obviously, Matthew is making it clear that Joseph is not the
father of Jesus. Although he is the husband of Mary, he is not the father
of Jesus.

What is the explanation of this? Well, Matthew in the rest of this
chapter will give us the explanation and will show how it fulfills Old
Testament prophecy.

THE VIRGIN BIRTH OF JESUS CHRIST

Luke, who wrote the Gospel bearing his name, was a Greek doctor. In
his Gospel, he goes into an extended section on obstetrics. Both Gospels declare that Jesus was virgin born. Joseph was not His father, but
Mary was not unfaithful to Joseph. Jesus is not an illegitimate child.
This is something new: ". . . A woman shall compass a man" (Jer.
31:22).

Now, my friend, I have never objected to any man saying that he does not believe in the virgin birth. A man has the right to disbelieve. But I do have two very definite objections: I do not think that a *preacher* should deny the virgin birth of Jesus Christ. If he does, then he ought to get a job selling insurance and deal with births in a different way. And I do object to anyone saying that the *Bible* does not teach the virgin birth of Christ. The only Jesus that we have any historical record of is the One who was virgin born. If you want to take the position that He was not virgin born, where is your documentation? You will have to produce evidence—certainly more than the puny reasoning of man. It is so easy to sit in a swivel chair in some theological seminary and write a thesis on the impossibility of the virgin birth. You may write a very profound tome on the subject, but you haven't any documents to back up your denial. All you have is just rationalism. By the process of rationalizing you may say, "It couldn't have happened." Well, who are you to say that it couldn't have happened? A few years ago man said that it was impossible to go to the moon, but we have gone there, and we have gone there by using the laws of God. God is the Creator of natural laws. He can either use those natural laws or He can set them aside in order to accomplish His purposes. The record clearly states that Jesus Christ was virgin born.

In verse 17 we find a statement which will explain something in the genealogies.

So all the generations from Abraham to David are fourteen generations; and from David until the carrying away into Babylon are fourteen generations; and from the carrying away into Babylon unto Christ are fourteen generations [Matt. 1:17].

Matthew puts the genealogy into groupings to give an overall view of Old Testament history. One era extends from Abraham to David, another from David to the Babylonian captivity, and the third from the captivity in Babylon to the birth of Jesus Christ. Obviously, he has omitted some names from the genealogy in order to fit fourteen into each period. The question is, why did he do this? Apparently, the number fourteen (twice seven) offered some proof concerning the accuracy of this genealogy.

Now that Matthew has shown that Joseph is not the father of Jesus, he is going to give us an explanation. Already in the Old Testament, a supernatural birth has been predicted by God. Jeremiah is talking to the nation Israel when he says, "How long wilt thou go about, O thou backsliding daughter? for the LORD hath created a new thing in the earth, A woman shall compass a man" (Jer. 31:22). That's not the way it's done, my friend. That's not natural birth; it's supernatural. The virgin birth of the Lord Jesus is the "new thing" which God has done. And it is the fulfillment of Jeremiah's prophecy.

> **Now the birth of Jesus Christ was on this wise: When as his mother Mary was espoused to Joseph, before they came together, she was found with child of the Holy Ghost [Matt. 1:18].**

"The birth of Jesus Christ was on this wise." Here's the way it happened, Matthew is telling us. When His mother, Mary, was espoused to Joseph, that is, she was engaged to him, before they came together—they had had no sexual relationship—she was found with child of the Holy Spirit.

> **Then Joseph her husband, being a just man, and not willing to make her a public example, was minded to put her away privily [Matt. 1:19].**

The Mosaic Law was very specific at this point. It said that a woman who was guilty of being unfaithful should be stoned to death—that was the extreme penalty. But this man Joseph was a remarkable man. We devote a great deal of attention to Mary, and rightly so. Protestants should not let themselves be deterred from giving Mary a great deal of credit. She was a remarkable person. Remember that she was the one whom God chose to be the mother of our Lord, and God makes no mistakes. He picked the right girl. While all of this is true, we need to remember that God also chose Joseph. God made no mistake in choosing him either. A hot-headed man would immediately have had her stoned to death or would have made her a public example by exposing her. But Joseph was not that kind of man. He was a gentle person. He was in *love* with her, and he did not want to hurt her in any way, although he felt that she had been unfaithful to him.

> **But while he thought on these things, behold, the angel of the Lord appeared unto him in a dream, saying, Joseph, thou son of David, fear not to take unto thee Mary thy wife: for that which is conceived in her is of the Holy Ghost [Matt. 1:20].**

In order to prevent a very tragic situation, the angel appeared to Joseph to make clear to him what was taking place.

> **And she shall bring forth a son, and thou shalt call his name JESUS: for he shall save his people from their sins [Matt. 1:21].**

The name *Jesus* means "Savior." He shall have the name Jesus because He shall save His people from their sins.

> **Now all this was done, that it might be fulfilled which was spoken of the Lord by the prophet, saying [Matt. 1:22].**

Matthew, who is writing for the nation Israel, points out that all this was done so that it might be fulfilled as the Lord had spoken. Matthew is appealing to the nation Israel to understand that this One who had come must be the fulfillment of the Old Testament prophecy.

It has been said that there are over three hundred prophecies concerning the first coming of Christ that have been literally fulfilled. I don't know how many of them are in Matthew, but I do know that Matthew quoted more from the Old Testament than the other three Gospel writers all together. It seems he records things and substantiates them from the Old Testament because he is not primarily trying to give a "life of Christ" but is showing that this is the fulfillment of the Old Testament prophecies concerning Him.

Now he states the prophecy which was given in Isaiah 7:14:

Behold, a virgin shall be with child, and shall bring forth a son, and they shall call his name Emmanuel, which being interpreted is, God with us [Matt. 1:23].

Now let's look at this a moment because it is very important. The liberal theologian has, of course, denied the fact of the virgin birth of Christ, and he has denied that the Bible teaches His virgin birth. Very candidly, I suspect that the Revised Standard Version was published in order to try to maintain some of the theses of the liberals. In fact, I am sure of this because one of the doctrines they have denied is the virgin birth. In the New Testament of the Revised Standard Version, which was copyrighted in 1946, Matthew 1:23 reads thus: "All this took place to fulfill what the Lord had spoken by the prophet: 'Behold, a virgin shall conceive and bear a son, and his name shall be called Emmanuel' (which means, God with us)."

In the Old Testament of the Revised Standard Version, which was copyrighted in 1952, Isaiah 7:14 reads like this: "Therefore the Lord himself will give you a sign. Behold, a young woman shall conceive and bear a son, and shall call his name Immanuel." Notice that in Isaiah they substituted "young woman" for the word *virgin*, even though in Matthew 1:23 they had used the word *virgin*, which is a fulfillment of Isaiah 7:14!

The prophecy of Isaiah 7:14 was given as a *sign*. My friend, it is no sign at all for a young woman to conceive and bear a son. If that's a sign, then right here in Southern California a sign is taking place many times a day, every day. They translated it "young woman" to tone down that word *virgin*.

Let us look at Isaiah 7:14 in the original Hebrew language. The word used for "virgin" is *almah*. The translators of the RSV went to the writings of Gesenius, an outstanding scholar who has an exhaustive Hebrew lexicon. (I can testify that it's also exhausting to look at it!) Gesenius admitted that the common translation of the word is "virgin," but he said that it could be changed to "young woman." The reason he said that was because he rejected the miraculous. So this new translation and others who have followed him, have attempted to say that *almah* means "young woman" and not "virgin."

Let's turn back to Isaiah 7 and study the incident recorded there. This was during the time when Ahaz was on the throne. He was one of those who was far from God, and I list him as a bad king. God sent Isaiah to bring a message to him, and he wouldn't listen. So we read: "Moreover the LORD spake again unto Ahaz, saying, Ask thee a sign of the LORD thy God; ask it either in the depth, or in the height above. But Ahaz said, I will not ask, neither will I tempt the LORD" (Isa. 7:10–12). May I say, it was pious hypocrisy for him to say what he did. God had asked Isaiah to meet Ahaz on the way to deliver God's message to him that God would give victory to Ahaz. However, Ahaz wouldn't believe God and so, in order to encourage his faith, Isaiah tells him that God wants to give him a sign. In his super-pious way Ahaz says, "Oh, I wouldn't ask a sign of the Lord." Isaiah answered him, "God is going to give you a sign whether you like it or not. The sign isn't just for you but for the whole house of David." Now here is the sign: ". . . Behold, a virgin shall conceive, and bear a son, and shall call his name Immanuel" (Isa. 7:14). Obviously, if this refers to a young woman, it would be no sign to Ahaz, or to the house of David, or to anybody else; but if a *virgin* conceives and bears a son, that, my friend, is a sign. And that's exactly what it means.

When the word *almah* is used in the Old Testament, it means a virgin. Rebekah was called an *almah* before she married Isaac. I asked a very fine Hebrew Christian, who is also a good Hebrew scholar, about that. He said, "Look at it this way. Suppose you went to visit a friend of yours who had three daughters and two of them were married and one was still single. He would say, 'These two are my married daughters, and this young lady is my third daughter.' Do you think he would mean a prostitute when he said 'young lady'? If you would imply that she was anything but a virgin, he would probably knock your block off." May I say, I would hate to be those who deny the virgin birth of Jesus Christ when they must come into the presence of the Son of God. I'm afraid they are going to wish they could somehow take back the things they have said to malign Him.

The fact that the word *almah* means "a virgin" is proven by the Septuagint. During the intertestamental period, seventy-two Hebrew scholars, six from each of the twelve tribes, worked down in Alexandria, Egypt, on the translation of the Hebrew Old Testament into the Greek language. When they came to this "sign" in Isaiah, those seventy-two men understood that it meant "virgin," and they translated it into the Greek word *parthenos*. That is the same word which Matthew uses in his Gospel. My friend, *parthenos* does not mean "young woman"; it means "virgin." For example, Athena was the virgin goddess of Athens, and her temple was called the Parthenon because *parthenos* means "virgin." It is clear that the Word of God is saying precisely what it means.

HIS NAME

Notice something wonderful. "Behold, a virgin shall be with child, and shall bring forth a son, and they shall call his name Emmanuel, which being interpreted is, God with us." It looks as if there is a problem here. Can you tell me where Jesus was ever called Emmanuel? No, He is called Jesus because that is His name. He was given this name because He shall save His people from their sins. Christ, by the way, is His title; Jesus is His name. But it says here that He shall be called "Emmanuel, which being interpreted is, God with us."

Friend, here we have one of the most wonderful things in the entire Word of God. Let's look at this. Emmanuel means "God with us." He can't be Emmanuel, God with us, unless he is virgin born. That's the only way! And notice, unless He is Emmanuel, He cannot be Jesus, the Savior. The reason they call Him Jesus, Savior, is because He is God with us. This truth about the One who came down to this earth is one of the most wonderful things in the Bible.

"But we see Jesus, who was made a little lower than the angels for the suffering of death, crowned with glory and honour; that he by the grace of God should taste death for every man" (Heb. 2:9). He had to be a sacrifice that was acceptable. I couldn't die for the sins of the world. I can't even die a redemptive death for my own sins. But He can! How can Jesus be a Savior? Because He is Emmanuel, God with us. How did He get with us? He was virgin born. I say again, He was called Jesus. He was never called Emmanuel. But you cannot call Him Jesus unless He is Emmanuel, God with us. He must be Emmanuel to be the Savior of the world. That is how important the virgin birth is.

Can a person be a Christian and deny the virgin birth? Hear me very carefully: I believe that it is possible to accept Christ as your Savior without knowing much about Him. You may not even know that this record is in the Bible. But after you have become a child of God, you will not deny the virgin birth of the Lord Jesus. You may not have to know it to be saved, but as a child of God you cannot deny the virgin birth of Jesus Christ.

Do I sound dogmatic, friend? Well, I hope I do because I consider this to be all-important. I want a Savior who is able to reach down and save Vernon McGee. If He's just another man like I am, then He's not going to be able to help me very much. But if He is Emmanuel, God with us, virgin born, then He is my Savior. Is He your Savior today? He took upon Himself our humanity in this way so that He might taste death for us, that He might die a redemptive death on the cross for us.

CHAPTER 2

THEME: *The visit of the wise men after the birth of the Lord Jesus; the flight into Egypt; the return to Nazareth*

THE FULFILLMENT OF PROPHECY

All of this is a historical record of what took place, but back of it there is a tremendous truth being presented, and we don't want to miss that. We have said before that each Gospel was directed to meet the needs of a particular group of people and that Matthew was written to the nation of Israel. It is for religious people. Recorded here is the fulfillment of four prophecies. To show how these Old Testament prophecies were fulfilled at the birth of Jesus is the purpose, I believe, of this chapter. I am sure there were many sincere students of the Scriptures living in Christ's day who wondered how all of these prophecies could be fulfilled. It seemed difficult, if not impossible. Let me list several here, then we will see how they were fulfilled at the time of Christ's birth: (1) He was to be born in Bethlehem (see Mic. 5:2); (2) He was to be called out of Egypt (see Hos. 11:1); (3) There was to be weeping in Ramah (see Jer. 31:15); and (4) He was a root from the stem of Jesse and therefore to be called a Nazarene (see Isa. 11:1).

Since Christ was to be born in Bethlehem, why should there be weeping in Ramah, which is about as far north of Jerusalem as Bethlehem is south of Jerusalem? And He was to be called a Nazarene although He would be born in Bethlehem and called out of Egypt. The question is: How could all of these prophecies be fulfilled in a little baby? Well, Matthew shows how literally, accurately, and easily all were fulfilled without any strain on prophecy or on history. It just came about as God said it would come about.

In our day when there are certain prophecies that relate to the second coming of Christ, we may find it difficult to correlate them and to see the way in which they can all be fulfilled. I'm of the opinion we are coming to the time of their fulfillment, and we are going to find out that it all will take place in a normal, natural way. It looks like a jigsaw puzzle to us down here, but, when we get into His presence and it is all fulfilled, it will have been just as natural as the prophecies about His first coming. Every little piece in the jigsaw puzzle will fit into place, and we're going to wonder why in the world we didn't see it at the time.

THE VISIT OF THE WISE MEN

Now when Jesus was born in Bethlehem of Judaea in the days of Herod the king, behold, there came wise men from the east to Jerusalem [Matt. 2:1].

This is the historical record of the coming of the wise men. Notice that they came in the days of Herod the king. One thing that Herod did not want was competition. In fact, the one thing that Herod would not *tolerate* was competition. So the wise men coming to Jerusalem really alerted him.

"Behold there came three wise men from the east to Jerusalem." Is that what your Bible says? You say, "No, you've inserted the number three." Well, isn't that what you've been taught by your Christmas cards? I think a great many people know more about the Christmas story from Christmas cards than from the Bible, and therefore they have many inaccurate impressions. I'll attempt to correct several of them in this chapter.

First, you will notice that the record doesn't tell us there were three wise men. I don't know how many there were, but I doubt whether three wise men would have disturbed Herod or have excited Jerusalem. I do believe that three hundred men would have done so. These wise men who came from the East evidently came from different areas. They had been studying the stars, and when this new star appeared, they joined forces and came to Jerusalem. I don't know how many there were, but I'm almost sure it wasn't three, and I believe three hundred would be more nearly true. But, please, don't say that I said there were three hundred!

But the wise men came—

Saying, Where is he that is born King of the Jews? for we have seen his star in the east, and are come to worship him [Matt. 2:2].

They were looking for a king, and that was the thing which disturbed Herod, the king.

"We have seen his star in the east." In poetry that is called the eastern star, and, actually, there is an organization by that name. The worthy matron of that group was a member of my church in Nashville, and she was greatly upset when she heard me say that it was not an eastern star. If they had seen His star in the east and it had been an eastern star, the wise men would have ended up in India or China. The star was in the west! The wise men were in the east. The star was in the west, and they followed it. They came west, not east. My question is this: How in the world did they associate a star with a king, and how did they identify it with Israel? All I know is that in that section of the East, the people had a prophecy given by Balaam, which is recorded in Numbers 24:17. (Remember that old Balaam gave this prophecy concerning the nation Israel.) "I shall see him, but not now: I shall behold him, but not nigh: there shall come a Star out of Jacob, and a Sceptre shall rise out of Israel, and shall smite the corners of Moab, and destroy all the children of Sheth."

Notice that the prophecy says a Star shall come out of Jacob—that is, the nation Israel. And a Sceptre shall rise out of Israel. The star and the sceptre go together. That is the only place I know where they are put together in prophecy in the Old Testament. The wise men in the East had that prophecy, and so they came out of the mysterious East seeking a king.

This did disturb the city of Jerusalem and old King Herod.

When Herod the king had heard these things, he was troubled, and all Jerusalem with him [Matt. 2:3].

When there converged on the city of Jerusalem a very impressive delegation of wise men, asking a question like this, the whole city was disturbed.

Herod wanted to know about this. This man was Herod the Great, a very superstitious man. I hope that you have a good Bible dictionary and that you will take time to read about the Herod family. They were a bunch of rascals, much like the house of de'Medici. This family was a real first century Mafia. Herod the Great was the biggest rascal of them all. He was an Idumean who had bought his position from the Roman government; he was not of Israel at all. And he was really anxious to locate this One who appeared to be a rival for his throne.

And when he had gathered all the chief priests and scribes of the people together, he demanded of them where Christ should be born [Matt. 2:4].

He didn't ask; he *demanded*. He said, "I know that you have the Scriptures and in them you have a record of a Messiah that is coming. I want to know where He is to be born." One of the amazing things is that they were able to tell him.

And they said unto him, In Bethlehem of Judaea: for thus it is written by the prophet,

And thou Bethlehem, in the land of Juda, art not the least among the princes of Juda: for out of thee shall come a Governor, that shall rule my people Israel [Matt. 2:5–6].

When Herod asked the scribes this question, they didn't have to search the Scriptures for it; they knew where it was—Micah 5:2. As a matter of fact, they didn't need even to turn to it, because they had it in their minds. They could quote it. They knew all about the coming of the Messiah. The problem was that their knowledge was academic rather than vital. It was not personally meaningful to them. They are examples of folk who know the history contained in the Bible and they know certain factual truths, but these things carry no personal meaning for them. Since the scribes knew the Old Testament Scriptures so well, you would have thought that they would have gone to the wise

men and said, "How about letting us ride down with you? We are
looking for the Messiah too!"

I wonder today how many people are really looking for the coming
of the Lord. We talk about it, and we study a great deal about prophecy. Would you really like to see Him right now? Suppose He broke in
right today where you are and into what you are doing. Would He
interrupt anything? Would you like to say to Him, "I wish that You
would postpone your visit to some other time"?

Herod got his information from the scribes—

> **Then Herod, when he had privily called the wise men,
> inquired of them diligently what time the star appeared
> [Matt. 2:7].**

I am going to make a statement now and will try to prove it later: The
star had appeared in the night sky sometime before the wise men appeared in Jerusalem. Remember that they made the trip by camel—not
by jet plane. It is a long, hard trip by camel! I am of the opinion that
they didn't arrive in Jerusalem until at least a year after the appearance of the star. This wasn't just a little Christmas celebration for
them. As they traveled the long, weary miles, they had been hanging
on to the hope of seeing Him and presenting their gifts to Him. Notice
that Herod "inquired diligently" the *time* of the star's appearance in
the sky. Keep that in mind. It will be an important fact later in the
story.

So Herod sends the wise men on to Bethlehem—

> **And he sent them to Bethlehem, and said, Go and
> search diligently for the young child; and when ye have
> found him, bring me word again, that I may come and
> worship him also [Matt. 2:8].**

He's being as subtle as an old serpent, and that's exactly what Herod
was. Suppose he had said, "If there's a king born around here, I'm
going to get rid of him," and then had sent soldiers down to Bethlehem. I can assure you that he would never have found the Child be-

cause He would have been hidden. He knew that the clever way and the best way was to let the wise men go down and find the child and then come back and tell him. He said he wanted to go down and worship Him, but of course what he really wanted to do was to kill Him.

> **When they had heard the king, they departed; and, lo, the star, which they saw in the east, went before them, till it came and stood over where the young child was.**

> **When they saw the star, they rejoiced with exceeding great joy [Matt. 2:9–10].**

Now the star appears again. I think they must have traveled a long time without seeing the star. That ought to answer the nonsense one hears today about there being a confluence of certain stars that happened at one particular time. Matthew makes it clear that this star was a very unusual star; in fact, it was a supernatural star. It was miraculous, and we needn't try to find an explanation for it. Now, it may be, as many astronomers think, that there was quite a movement in the heavens at that time. When He came, heaven and earth both responded to His coming into this world. I think such things did take place, but the wise men saw a supernatural star.

> **And when they were come into the house, they saw the young child with Mary his mother, and fell down, and worshipped him: and when they had opened their treasures, they presented unto him gifts; gold, and frankincense, and myrrh [Matt. 2:11].**

When they arrived, Jesus was not in the stable behind an inn. The great movement of people in the city of Bethlehem had now all ceased. They had gone back to their homes because the enrollment was over. But this little Baby was newly born, and they couldn't move Him for a while. Probably such a trip for the Little One would have jeopardized His life. So they had stayed in Bethlehem and had moved into a house. The wise men found them in a house. Again, the Christmas cards show the wise men coming into the stable. Well, unless Joseph pointed out that stable to them, they never even knew where it was. They came to the *house*.

Please note that when they saw the young child with Mary His mother, they fell down and worshiped Him. If ever there was a time when Mary should have been worshiped, this was it. But they didn't worship her—they were *wise* men! They worshiped Him and presented to Him their treasures: gold and frankincense and myrrh.

It is very interesting to study the facts concerning His second coming as they are related to us in Isaiah 60:6: "The multitude of camels shall cover thee, the dromedaries of Midian and Ephah, all they from Sheba shall come: they shall bring gold and incense; and they shall shew forth the praises of the LORD." What gift is left out at His second coming? Myrrh! They do not bring myrrh because that speaks of His death. When He comes the second time, nothing will speak of His death. Gold speaks of His birth. He is born a King. Frankincense speaks of the fragrance of His life. Myrrh speaks of His death. All of this is indicated in the gifts that were brought to Him at His first coming. But at His next coming, myrrh will not be brought to Him. The next time He comes, He won't come to die upon a cross for the sins of the world. He will come as King of kings and Lord of lords.

> **And being warned of God in a dream that they should not return to Herod, they departed into their own country another way [Matt. 2:12].**

The wise men had assumed that Herod was sincere and wanted to come down and worship Him. However, he would have killed the Child had not an angel of the Lord warned the wise men to go back to their own country by a different route. They may have continued south down to Hebron, then crossed over south of the Dead Sea, and thus they would be out of the range of Herod altogether.

THE FLIGHT INTO EGYPT

> **And when they were departed, behold, the angel of the Lord appeareth to Joseph in a dream, saying, Arise, and**

**take the young child and his mother, and flee into Egypt,
and be thou there until I bring thee word; for Herod will
seek the young child to destroy him [Matt. 2:13].**

The angel of the Lord appeared also to Joseph and told him that it was
time to get the Child out of Bethlehem because Herod would attempt
to murder Him.

**When he arose, he took the young child and his mother
by night, and departed into Egypt [Matt. 2:14].**

Notice Joseph's instant obedience.

**And was there until the death of Herod: that it might be
fulfilled which was spoken of the Lord by the prophet,
saying, Out of Egypt have I called my son [Matt. 2:15].**

This is a quotation from Hosea 11:1. This is a marvelous prophecy
because it has a historical basis. Out of Egypt the son was called,
which was the *nation;* and out of Egypt the Son was called, who was a
Person, this Child. So Joseph took the young Child and the mother to
Egypt and stayed there until God called Him out.

**Then Herod, when he saw that he was mocked of the
wise men, was exceeding wroth, and sent forth, and
slew all the children that were in Bethlehem, and in all
the coasts thereof, from two years old and under, according to the time which he had diligently inquired of
the wise men [Matt. 2:16].**

Part of what I'm going to say now is supposition, and part is based on
solid fact. As I mentioned before, the wise men did not arrive at the
time the shepherds arrived at the stable. The wise men came later,
and, according to verse 11, the family had moved into a house by then.
When Herod had had his private session with the wise men, he "inquired of them diligently what time the star appeared." I suppose that

the wise men said, "Well, it was about a year ago." If we are accurate in thinking that these wise men came from all quarters of the East and had met in a certain place from which they began their trek to Jerusalem, that would consume a great deal of time in a day when travel was by camel instead of by jet. It may have been a year, it may have been longer, but Herod was so infuriated that the wise men did not come back and report concerning the Child, that he probably said, "Well, if they said it was a year ago when they saw the star, I'll just double it and make it two years and kill all the children two years old and younger!" Herod was actually a madman.

Then was fulfilled that which was spoken by Jeremy the prophet, saying,

In Rama was there a voice heard, lamentation, and weeping, and great mourning, Rachel weeping for her children, and would not be comforted, because they are not [Matt. 2:17–18].

This is an unusual prophecy also. Jeremiah didn't say that the weeping would be heard in Bethlehem. I'm sure there was great mourning in Bethlehem too. But Jeremiah mentions Rama (spelled Ramah in the Old Testament), and Rama was about as far north of Jerusalem as Bethlehem was south of Jerusalem. And Rama was Jeremiah's country, by the way. I imagine that when the soldiers had been given their orders to slay the children, the captain said to Herod, "Where do you want me to begin?" And I think that old Herod said, "Well, just draw a circle around Jerusalem with the radius as far south as Bethlehem and as far north as Rama"—yet Rama was not in any way involved in it. So, you see, Herod slew a great many children. You can imagine the weeping all the way from Bethlehem to Rama, a radius of about ten to twelve miles, or twenty to twenty-five miles across the area. It must have been a heartbreaking time in the lives of these people when they lost their little ones. The prophecy given through Jeremiah was literally fulfilled.

THE RETURN TO NAZARETH

But when Herod was dead, behold, an angel of the Lord appeareth in a dream to Joseph in Egypt [Matt. 2:19].

I must call attention to this. We are told that *the* angel of the Lord appeared to Jacob at Peniel (see Gen. 32). Here it is *an* angel of the Lord. *The* angel of the Lord is the pre-incarnate Christ. Now Christ incarnate is down in Egypt.

Saying, Arise, and take the young child and his mother, and go into the land of Israel: for they are dead which sought the young child's life [Matt. 2:20].

It's essential to get Jesus out of the land of Egypt and back up into Israel. The most important reason is that He has been born under the Law, and He is to live under the Mosaic Law. He is the only One who really ever kept it. He must get out from under the influence of Egypt. He is not to be raised down there as Moses had been and as the children of Israel had been when they were becoming a nation down in Egypt.

And he arose, and took the young child and his mother, and came into the land of Israel.

But when he heard that Archelaus did reign in Judaea in the room of his father Herod, he was afraid to go thither: notwithstanding, being warned of God in a dream, he turned aside into the parts of Galilee [Matt. 2:21–22].

By the way, Archelaus was another Herod and very brutal.

And he came and dwelt in a city called Nazareth: that it might be fulfilled which was spoken by the prophets, He shall be called a Nazarene [Matt. 2:23].

"He shall be called a Nazarene." The Hebrew word for Nazareth was *Netzer,* meaning a branch or shoot. The city of Nazareth was so called because of its insignificance. The prophecies of Isaiah 11:1; Isaiah 53:2–3; and Psalm 22:6 are involved in the term *Nazarene.* But the Lord Jesus was given that term not only because He was a root out of the stem of Jesse, but because He grew up in the city of Nazareth, and He was called a Nazarene, which fulfilled the prophecies.

Now we have seen all four of the prophecies dealing with locations in the birth of Christ: born in Bethlehem, called out of Egypt, weeping in Rama, and called a Nazarene were fulfilled in a very normal way. He touched base in all of these places, and what seemed rather strange prophecies became very sane realities.

CHAPTER 3

THEME: John the Baptist, the forerunner of the King, announces the Kingdom and baptizes Jesus, the King

MINISTRY OF JOHN THE BAPTIST

In those days came John the Baptist, preaching in the wilderness of Judaea,

And saying, Repent ye: for the kingdom of heaven is at hand [Matt. 3:1–2].

Now, all of a sudden, John the Baptist walks onto the pages of Scripture. If we had Matthew's Gospel only, we would ask, "Where did he come from, and what is his background?"—because Matthew gives us none of that, and the reason is obvious. The prophet Malachi had said that the messenger would come ahead to prepare the way for the coming of the King—"Behold, I will send my messenger, and he shall prepare the way before me . . ." (Mal. 3:1). This messenger was John the Baptist. You don't really need to know about the background of a messenger. When the Western Union boy delivers a message to your door, do you say to him, "Young man, did your ancestors come over on the Mayflower? What is your background?" You're not interested in that. You are interested in the message because the message is all-important, and that is what you want. So you thank him, give him a tip, and dismiss him. You are through with him.

John the Baptist made it very clear that he was just the messenger, and Matthew is making that clear, too. Therefore, he walks out onto the page of Scripture, preaching in the wilderness of Judea saying, "Repent ye: for the kingdom of heaven is at hand."

Now let's deal with these expressions: (1) "Repent ye"; (2) "the kingdom of heaven"; and (3) "is at hand." They are very important.

"Repent" is an expression that always has been given to God's people as a challenge to turn around. "Repent" in the original Greek is *metanoia,* meaning "to change your mind." You are going in one direction; turn around and go in another direction.

Repentance is primarily, I think, for saved people, that is, for God's people in any age. They are the ones who, when they become cold and indifferent, are to turn. That was the message to the seven churches of Asia Minor in Revelation 2 and 3, and it was the message of the Lord Jesus Himself.

Someone may ask whether the unsaved man is supposed to repent. The unsaved man is told that he is to *believe* on the Lord Jesus Christ. That was the message of Paul to the jailer at Philippi (see Acts 16:31). That old rascal needed to do some repenting; but when an unsaved man believes in Jesus, he is repenting. Faith means to turn to Christ, and when you turn to Christ, you must also turn from something. If you don't turn from something, then you aren't really turning to Christ. So repentance is really a part of believing, but the primary message that should be given to the lost today is that they should *believe* in the Lord Jesus Christ. We like to see folk come forward in a service to receive Christ or sign a card signifying that they have made that decision, but the important thing is to *trust* Christ as your Savior, and if you really turn *to* Him, you turn *from* something else.

The expression "kingdom of heaven" means the rule of the heavens over the earth. The Lord Jesus is the King. You can't have a kingdom without a king; neither can you have a king without a kingdom. Remember Richard III who said in the Shakespearean play, "My kingdom for a horse." If he had traded his kingdom for a horse, he wouldn't have been a king. He would have been only a man on horseback. A king must have a kingdom. So what did John the Baptist mean by "the kingdom of heaven is at hand"? He meant that the Kingdom of Heaven is present in the Person of the King.

Is there a present reality of the Kingdom of Heaven? Yes, there is. Those who come to Him as Savior and acknowledge Him are translated into the Kingdom of His dear Son. They belong to Him now. And they have a much more intimate relationship than that of a subject with a king. Christ is the Bridegroom, and believers are part of His bride!

Then someone may ask whether we are like subjects in a kingdom because we are to carry out His commands. Again I say, there is more to it than that. We are to obey Him because we love Him. It is a love relationship. "If ye love me, keep my commandments" (John 14:15).

The "kingdom of heaven" is the rule of the heavens over the earth. That's not in existence today. Christ is not reigning over the world now. There must be something wrong with the thinking of those who insist that the Kingdom of Heaven is in existence in our day. Christ is not reigning in any form, shape, or fashion—except in the hearts of those who have received Him. However, He is coming someday to establish His Kingdom on the earth. When He does, He will put down rebellion. Believe me, He is really going to put it down.

The Kingdom of Heaven was at hand, or was present, in the Person of the King. That was the only way in which it was present.

Matthew now tells us that what he is recording is in fulfillment of prophecy—

> **For this is he that was spoken of by the prophet Esaias, saying, The voice of one crying in the wilderness, Prepare ye the way of the Lord, make his paths straight [Matt. 3:3].**

"The prophet Esaias" is Isaiah, and the prophecy is in Isaiah 40:3.

"The voice of one crying in the wilderness"—all that John the Baptist claimed for himself was that he was a voice crying in the wilderness. And his purpose was to "prepare the way of the Lord."

> **And the same John had his raiment of camel's hair, and a leathern girdle about his loins; and his meat was locusts and wild honey [Matt. 3:4].**

He's a strange individual, isn't he? He follows a strange diet and has an unusual way of dressing. I hate to say this, but today John would probably qualify in his looks as a vagrant. His raiment was of camel's hair, his leathern girdle was about his loins, his meat was locusts and wild honey. We're told that he never shaved and had long hair. Here's an unusual man, friend, a man with a mission. He's really an Old

Testament character, walking out of the Old Testament onto the pages of the New Testament. He is the last of the Old Testament prophets.

Then went out to him Jerusalem, and all Judaea, and all the region round about Jordan [Matt. 3:5].

Notice that the crowds went out to him. John did not rent a stadium or an auditorium or a church, and there was no committee that invited him. In fact, he didn't come to town at all. If you wanted to hear John, you went out to where he was. Obviously, the Spirit of God was on this man.

And were baptized of him in Jordan, confessing their sins [Matt. 3:6].

In other words, all of this denoted a *change* in the lives of these people. The very fact that they submitted to John's baptism was an indication that they were leaving their old lives and turning to new lives.

THE PHARISEES AND SADDUCEES

But when he saw many of the Pharisees and Sadducees come to his baptism, he said unto them, O generation of vipers, who hath warned you to flee from the wrath to come?

Bring forth therefore fruits meet for repentance [Matt. 3:7–8].

Now see who is coming! Listen to the way he greets these dignified visitors. Suppose your preacher got up next Sunday morning and said, "O generation of vipers"! I imagine that the deacons would be looking for another preacher! This is really strong language. He's talking to the dignified Pharisees and Sadducees and is telling them, "There must be evidence of this new life. You can't just go through the *act* of baptism. There must be fruit in your life."

> And think not to say within yourselves, We have Abraham to our father: for I say unto you, that God is able of these stones to raise up children unto Abraham [Matt. 3:9].

Friend, he's making a strong statement here! You can understand why he was not elected the most popular man of the year in Judea.

> And now also the axe is laid unto the root of the trees: therefore every tree which bringeth not forth good fruit is hewn down, and cast into the fire [Matt. 3:10].

A great deal is said in the New Testament about fruit bearing. Fruit bearing is the result of having the right kind of tree. Only a fruit tree can produce fruit. He talks here about the axe being laid to the root of the tree, and the reason is that the tree is not bearing fruit. An apple tree will bear apples, and a plum tree will bear plums. But when a tree bears thorns, it is not an apple tree, and it must be cut down. The root and the fruit go together, by the way, and a tree must have the right kind of root to bear the right kind of fruit. That is exactly what John the Baptist is saying to them here. He is telling them that the wrong kind of tree is going to be taken down and cast into the fire.

> I indeed baptize you with water unto repentance: but he that cometh after me is mightier than I, whose shoes I am not worthy to bear: he shall baptize you with the Holy Ghost, and with fire [Matt. 3:11].

John is saying, "l baptize with water. But He is coming, and when He comes, He will baptize you with the Holy Ghost, and with fire"—that final "and" is already over nineteen hundred years long. You and I are living in the age of the Holy Spirit. Christ Jesus baptizes with the Holy Spirit in this present age. He will baptize with fire when He comes the second time, and fire means judgment. This distinction needs to be made.

Somebody will say, "I thought that on the Day of Pentecost, the believers were baptized with the Holy Spirit and with fire, because it says that tongues of fire sat upon each of them." Oh, my friend, you ought to read Acts 2:2–3 again. The record is this: "And suddenly there came a sound from heaven *as* of a rushing mighty wind, and it filled all the house where they were sitting. And there appeared unto them cloven tongues *like as* of fire, and it sat upon each of them" (italics mine). It wasn't wind and it wasn't fire; it was the coming of the Holy Spirit. But there was something to appeal to the eye-gate and to the ear-gate. Therefore, when the Holy Spirit came, there was not the fulfillment of the baptism of fire. Let me repeat that, the baptism of fire will take place at the *second* coming of Christ. In the present age of the Holy Spirit, the Holy Spirit comes upon every believer. Not just *some*, but *every* believer is baptized by the Holy Spirit, which means that the believer is identified with the body of Christ; that is, he becomes part of the body of Christ. This is one of the great truths in the Word of God.

John continues to speak of Christ's second coming—

> **Whose fan is in his hand, and he will throughly purge his floor, and gather his wheat into the garner; but he will burn up the chaff with unquenchable fire [Matt. 3:12].**

JESUS IS BAPTIZED OF JOHN

> **Then cometh Jesus from Galilee to Jordan unto John, to be baptized of him [Matt. 3:13].**

This is remarkable, and we are going to ask the question: "Why was Jesus baptized?" and try to answer it.

> **But John forbad him, saying, I have need to be baptized of thee, and comest thou to me?**

> **And Jesus answering said unto him, Suffer it to be so now: for thus it becometh us to fulfil all righteousness. Then he suffered him [Matt. 3:14–15].**

Why was Jesus baptized? There may be several answers, but the primary reason is stated right here: "For thus it becometh us to fulfil all righteousness." Jesus is identifying Himself *completely* with sinful mankind. Isaiah had prophesied that He would be numbered with the transgressors (see Isa. 53:12). Here is a King who identifies Himself with His subjects. Actually, baptism means identification, and I believe identification was the primary purpose for the baptism of the Lord Jesus. Again, the reason Jesus was baptized was not to set an example for us. It was not a pattern for us to follow. Christ was holy— He did not need to repent. You and I do need to repent. He was holy, harmless, undefiled, and separate from sinners. He was baptized to completely identify Himself with humanity.

There was a second reason Jesus was baptized. Water baptism is symbolic of death. His death was a baptism. You remember that He said to James and John when they wanted to be seated on His right hand and on His left hand in the Kingdom, "Ye know not what ye ask. Are ye able to drink of the cup that I shall drink of, and to be baptized with the baptism that I am baptized with?" (Matt. 20:22). You see, Christ's death was a baptism. He entered into death for you and for me.

There is a third reason for the baptism of Jesus. At this time He was set aside for His office of priest. The Holy Spirit came upon Him for this priestly ministry. Everything that Jesus did, His every act, was done by the power of the Holy Spirit. "For he hath made him to be sin for us, who knew no sin; that we might be made the righteousness of God in him" (2 Cor. 5:21). There was sin on Him, but there was no sin in Him. My sin was put on Him, not in Him. That is an important distinction. Therefore, you and I are saved by being identified with Him. He identified Himself with us in baptism. And Peter says that we are saved by baptism (see 1 Pet. 3:21). In what way? By being identified with the Lord Jesus. To be saved is to be in Christ. How do we get into Christ? By the baptism of the Holy Spirit. I believe in water baptism because by it we declare that we are identified with Christ. The Lord Jesus said, ". . . him that cometh to me I will in no wise cast out" (John 6:37). We must recognize that we have to be identified with Christ, and that is accomplished by the Holy Spirit. Our water baptism is a testimony to this. One time an old salt said to a young sailor in trying to get him to accept Christ and be baptized, "Young man it is *duty* or *mutiny!*" And when you come to Christ, my friend, you are to be baptized because it is a duty. If you are not, it is mutiny.

This subject of baptism needs to be lifted out of the realm of argument to the high and lofty plane of standing for Christ. How we need to come out and stand for Christ!

Let me repeat verse 15: "And Jesus answering said unto him, Suffer it to be so now: for thus it becometh us to fulfil all righteousness. Then he suffered him"—that is, John baptized Him.

> **And Jesus, when he was baptized, went up straightway out of the water: and, lo, the heavens were opened unto him, and he saw the Spirit of God descending like a dove, and lighting upon him:**
>
> **And lo a voice from heaven, saying, This is my beloved Son, in whom I am well pleased [Matt. 3:16–17].**

Here we have a manifestation of the Trinity. As the Lord Jesus is coming out of the water, the Spirit of God descends upon Him like a dove, and the Father speaks from heaven.

The Father says, "This is my beloved Son, in whom I am well pleased." The Lord Jesus is now identified with His people. What a King! Oh, what a King He is!

CHAPTER 4

THEME: The temptation of Jesus in the wilderness, the beginning of His public ministry at Capernaum; the calling of four of His disciples by the Sea of Galilee

THE THREEFOLD TEMPTATION OF JESUS

Let us follow the movement of the Gospel of Matthew. Jesus came down to be born among us and so to be identified with us. He grew up as any other child would, except that He was harmless and without sin. Now, in His baptism, He has been identified with us. He has put on our sin. Now He is going to be tested because there are some real questions to be answered. Is the King able to withstand a test, and can He overcome?

The word *tempt* has a twofold meaning:

1. "Incite or entice to evil; seduce." There is something in each of us which causes us to yield to evil. This was not true of Jesus. ". . . the prince of this world cometh, and hath nothing in me" (John 14:30). He was ". . . holy, harmless, undefiled, separate from sinners . . ." (Heb. 7:26). So the temptation for Jesus had to be different from that which would cause me to fall, in that it needed to be a much greater temptation.

2. "Test." God does not tempt men with evil according to James 1:13. Yet, we are told ". . . God did tempt Abraham . . ." (Gen. 22:1). This means that God was testing the faith of Abraham.

Jesus is now to be tested. Could Jesus have fallen? I want to answer that with an emphatic *no!* He could not have fallen. If Jesus could have fallen, then you and I do not have a sure Savior at all.

Perhaps you are asking, "Well then, if Jesus could not have fallen, was His temptation a legitimate and genuine temptation?" May I say to you that His temptation was much greater than any that you and I have ever had. When a new model Chevrolet or Ford or Dodge is developed, it is thoroughly tested to prove it can stand the test. And every genuine diamond is tested to show that it is not a phony. In a similar way, the Lord Jesus Christ was tested to demonstrate that He was exactly who He claimed to be.

Let me illustrate with this little story. When I was a boy, I lived out in West Texas. It was a sparsely populated area in those days. The Santa Fe railroad came through our little town, but it went on by and stopped in the next little town. But it crossed the left fork of the Brazos River near our town. In the summertime there wasn't enough water in that river to rust a shingle nail, but in wintertime you could float a battleship on it. One winter we really had a flood, and it washed out the Santa Fe bridge. We were without a train for a long time. Finally, they put in a bridge. They worked a long time on it. Then one day they brought in two engines, stopped them on the bridge, and tied down their whistles. Believe me, that was more whistling than we had ever heard in our little town! All twenty-three of us ran down to see what was happening. As we were standing around, one brave citizen went up to the engineer in charge with our question, "What are you doing?" The engineer answered, "Testing the bridge." Our man said, "Are you trying to break it down?" The engineer almost sneered, "Of course not! We're testing it to *prove* that it can't be broken down."

May I say to you, that was the exact reason the Lord Jesus was tested. It was to prove, to demonstrate, that He could not be broken down. His testing, therefore, was greater than ours. There is a limit to what we can bear. You give me enough temptation, you build up the pressure, and finally I'll succumb to it. That is true of you too. But Christ never gave in although the pressure continued to increase. In other words, a ten-pound fishing line will break when twenty pounds of pressure is put on it, but a hundred-pound line can bear more than twenty-five pounds of pressure. Now, I'm the ten-pound fishing line, and He is the one hundred-pound line.

Another really interesting feature of this temptation is the comparison and contrast with the testing of Eve in the Garden of Eden. To begin with, Christ was tested in a wilderness while Eve was tested in a garden. What a contrast!

Then was Jesus led up of the Spirit into the wilderness to be tempted of the devil [Matt. 4:1].

He was to be *tested* by the Devil.

> **And when he had fasted forty days and forty nights, he was afterward an hungred.**

> **And when the tempter came to him, he said, If thou be the Son of God, command that these stones be made bread [Matt. 4:2–3].**

This is the same kind of temptation that came to Eve. The first one was *physical*. She saw that the tree was good for food (see Gen. 3:6). The Lord Jesus was told to turn stones to bread. First John 2:15–16 says that such temptation for the Christian is the ". . . lust of the flesh."

> **But he answered and said, It is written, Man shall not live by bread alone, but by every word that proceedeth out of the mouth of God [Matt. 4:4].**

That is found in Deuteronomy 8:3. Jesus surely knew Deuteronomy, and He believed it was the inspired Word of God.

Now the second testing:

> **Then the devil taketh him up into the holy city, and setteth him on a pinnacle of the temple,**

> **And saith unto him, If thou be the Son of God, cast thyself down: for it is written, He shall give his angels charge concerning thee: and in their hands they shall bear thee up, lest at any time thou dash thy foot against a stone [Matt. 4:5–6].**

The Devil is quoting Psalm 91:11–12, although he does not quote it accurately. Now, this is the *spiritual* temptation. For Eve it was that she saw the fruit was ". . . to be desired to make one wise . . ." (Gen. 3:6). For the Christian, it is the ". . . pride of life . . ." (1 John 2:16).

> **Jesus said unto him, It is written again, Thou shalt not tempt the Lord thy God [Matt. 4:7].**

He is quoting Deuteronomy 6:16.

The third testing is *psychological*.

> **Again, the devil taketh him up into an exceeding high mountain, and sheweth him all the kingdoms of the world, and the glory of them;**
>
> **And saith unto him, All these things will I give thee, if thou wilt fall down and worship me [Matt. 4:8–9].**

Satan showed Him the kingdoms of the world and their glory. This, you see, is a psychological temptation. Man lusts for power. Eve was subjected to the same temptation: ". . . ye shall be as gods, knowing good and evil" (Gen. 3:5). Many of us succumb to this test.

Notice the answer of the Lord Jesus—

> **Then saith Jesus unto him, Get thee hence, Satan: for it is written, Thou shalt worship the Lord thy God, and him only shalt thou serve [Matt. 4:10].**

He is quoting Deuteronomy 6:13 and 10:20. Friend, we see that our Lord answered each time with Scripture. Certainly, that ought to have a message for all of us.

Why is it that many of us are having trouble living the Christian life? May I say this very kindly: It is *ignorance* of the Word of God. Notice that our Lord always answered by giving the Word of God. I believe that the Word of God has an answer for your particular problem. That doesn't mean that *I* know the answer for your problem. It doesn't mean that your psychologist or psychiatrist knows the answer for your problem. But God has an answer for your problem, and it is in His Word. That is the reason we should know the Book better than we do.

Let me repeat, the Lord Jesus answered Satan every time out of the Word. He did not say, "Well, *I* think this" or "*I* believe there is a better way of doing it." He said very definitely that the Word of God says thus and so. He used the Word of God for His answer. And for the child of God, that is enough.

By the way, the Devil seemed to think it gave good answers because in the next verse we read—

Then the devil leaveth him, and behold, angels came and ministered unto him [Matt. 4:11].

Luke 4:13 tells us that the Devil left Him for a little season. I think he was back the next day—and was testing Him throughout His life. Especially do we see the temptation of the Devil in the Garden of Gethsemane where Jesus endured indescribable suffering.

Now let's make a very brief recapitulation of this episode in the life of our Lord and notice some things that it clearly teaches.

First of all, we have seen that Jesus was born a King, He was introduced as a King, He was baptized as a King, and now we have seen that He was tested as a King. All the way through Matthew's Gospel He is a King.

This testing revealed several things. One of them is that the Devil is a person. In this contact with Jesus, he is treated as a person. This ought to answer any Bible believer who has questions about him, because there are those who insist that the Devil is only an influence.

Also, we notice the very subtle insinuation of the Devil. He first said, "*If* thou be the Son of God, command that these stones be made bread" (v. 3). In other words, *prove* it in a way which is not God's way. There was no attempt, of course, to tempt Jesus to commit a crime. For Him, that would not have been a real temptation because the inclination of Jesus was to do good. Since bread was the staff of life, to make stones into bread would be a very good thing. And later on in His ministry He fed the multitudes with bread. But the inherent evil of Satan's temptation was to get Jesus to go outside of the will of God for His life.

Also, we see that all the way through the temptations, the Lord Jesus answered the Devil from the Word of God. In other words, He

used the sword of the Spirit (see Eph. 6:17) to meet the enemy of God
and man. Every time His answer was, "It is written." Oh, my friend, if
only we were more adept at using the sword of the Spirit! It is our
weapon in this day, and it is a very effective weapon.

Another interesting point is that Jesus quoted from the Book of
Deuteronomy.

The second thing the Devil wanted Jesus to do was to become a
religious leader by a stupendous miracle rather than by offering His
credentials in the manner that God had prescribed. The Devil's way
would miss the Cross of Christ. Much of what is called Christianity
today is "Devil-anity" or "Satan-anity" because it leaves the Cross of
Christ out altogether. The Devil is asking Jesus to become a great religious leader by a miracle.

Friend, it's very dangerous today to be led astray by miracle workers. Right now many people are going after so-called faith healers. I
don't know why so many folk go after that type of thing when a little
investigation would reveal that there are no real miracles taking place
in their services, although there is a great deal of emotion and folderol
involved. In Southern California I have made an offer of one hundred
dollars to anyone who will come forward and present their credentials
and demonstrate that they were actually healed by a miracle worker, a
healer. Frankly, I have been amazed that only two or three have come.
These were very sincere folk who really believed that they had been
healed. They thought that I was way out in left field because I didn't
believe they had been healed—and I didn't. But don't misunderstand,
I believe in miracle healing—that is, I believe that you go directly to
the Great Physician. When you have something seriously wrong with
you, you don't go to an intern or a quack doctor. What you do is go to a
specialist in that particular field. I've taken my case to the Great Physician, and I can recommend Him. I believe in going directly to Him
and not through some of these so-called miracle-workers. No man can
perform miracles. Not even the Lord Jesus would become a religious
leader the way the Devil wanted Him to become one, and that is very
interesting.

You'll notice that the Devil came back and quoted Scripture also.
He said: "For he shall give his angels charge over thee. . . . They shall

bear thee up in their hands, lest thou dash thy foot against a stone" (Ps. 91:11–12). The Devil was pretty good at quoting Scripture, but he wasn't quite accurate. Shakespeare said that the Devil could quote Scripture for his purpose; but, actually, the Devil can *misquote* Scripture for his purpose. Satan left out a very important phrase from the passage which he quoted from Psalm 91. He omitted ". . . to keep thee in all thy ways" (Ps. 91:11). That is the important part of the verse. Satan was attempting to get the Lord Jesus to ignore God's way. My friend, it is not always God's will to perform something in your life or in my life that is miraculous. There is an idea circulating in our contemporary society that we can *force* God to do something, that He is sort of a Western Union boy or that He is more or less working for you and is under your command to do what you desire Him to do. Oh, my friend, we can't do that! God is sovereign, and we happen to be the creature—He is the Creator. We must yield to the will of God. That may not be pleasant at times, but the will of God—not your will or my will—is that which is all important.

Another thing about this temptation which really raises a question is that the Devil offered the Lord Jesus the kingdoms of this world! Does the Devil have the kingdoms of the world to offer? Think that one over before you attempt to answer it. Well, let me give you my answer, and I have thought about it a great deal. The Lord Jesus did not challenge his statement that he had the kingdoms of the world to offer. Jesus didn't say to him, "You can't offer Me the kingdoms of the world because you don't have them to give." I assume that the Devil did have them to give. This fact gives us a little different viewpoint of the trouble we are having in the world today. The Devil is running everything! Some Christians tend to fight the evils of communism without realizing that behind communism is Satan and that behind the confusion and turmoil in the world is Satan. Let's remember who our enemy really is. He is a spiritual enemy. He wants to become God. Remember that he said to Jesus, "All these things will I give thee, if thou wilt fall down and *worship me*"!

In verse 11 we saw that after the third temptation, the Devil left the Lord Jesus for awhile. Certainly, he did not leave Him alone permanently.

JESUS BEGINS HIS PUBLIC
MINISTRY AT CAPERNAUM

Now when Jesus had heard that John was cast into prison, he departed into Galilee;

And leaving Nazareth, he came and dwelt in Capernaum, which is upon the sea coast, in the borders of Zabulon and Nephthalim [Matt. 4:12–13].

Jesus withdrew from the Jerusalem area because John had been taken by Herod and put in prison. Now we have the Lord Jesus shifting His headquarters from the south to the north and from Nazareth, His hometown, over to Capernaum. Matthew does not give us the details of this move in his record. This is an example of the fact that the four Gospel records do not attempt to parallel each other. One is not a carbon copy of any of the others. The attempt to harmonize the Gospels is a big mistake. I have written a booklet entitled *Why Four Gospels?* in which I attempt to show that each one is written for a definite purpose. Not one of them was intended to be a biography of the Lord Jesus—no one could write that. Each book presents its case to reach a certain segment of the human family. Matthew was written to reach the religious element and is primarily for the nation of Israel. Actually, it was written in Hebrew—Papias and Eusebius, church fathers, both say that, as well as others of that period.

Although Matthew gives us no details of the move to Capernaum, we learn from other Gospels that Jesus had been rejected by His hometown. Capernaum became His headquarters and continued as such, as far as we can tell, until the hour that He went to Jerusalem for the final time to be crucified.

Matthew will give us the reason He moved His headquarters from Nazareth to Capernaum. The other Gospel writers do not tell us this, but Matthew records it to show that in everything the Lord Jesus did, He was moving in fulfillment of the Old Testament prophecies—

That it might be fulfilled which was spoken by Esaias the prophet, saying,

The land of Zabulon, and the land of Nephthalim, by the way of the sea, beyond Jordan, Galilee of the Gentiles;

The people which sat in darkness saw great light; and to them which sat in the region and shadow of death light is sprung up [Matt. 4:14–16].

We find this prophecy in Isaiah 9:1–2 and Isaiah 42:6–7. I won't take the space to go into the background of this area called Galilee of the Gentiles, but if you want to do some research, you will find it very profitable to see the condition of that area at the time the Lord Jesus was there. Remember that He also spent His boyhood there. It was called Gentile country because out of the Roman Empire many folk had migrated to that area. There was a marvelous resort section around the Sea of Galilee, but it was very worldly and even wicked. The people in that area were very far from God.

The great light of the Lord Jesus broke upon them, and His very presence created a responsibility for them. They witnessed many of His miracles, but there was little response. Later, in Matthew 11:20–24, He pronounces judgment upon them when He says, "Woe unto thee, Chorazin!"

In Capernaum Jesus picked up right where John the Baptist left off.

From that time Jesus began to preach, and to say, Repent: for the kingdom of heaven is at hand [Matt. 4:17].

Jesus message was, "Repent, turn around, come to Me, the kingdom of heaven is at hand." It was at hand in the person of the King, of course—they couldn't have the Kingdom of Heaven without Him. As we have seen the Kingdom of Heaven, simply stated, is the reign of the heavens over the earth. This is what the Lord Jesus will bring to this earth someday. This earth will become "heaven" for Israel, an earthly people, and they will go into eternity right down here. The church has a heavenly hope, but the earthly hope is also a marvelous hope, and it is the hope of the Old Testament.

JESUS BEGINS TO CALL HIS DISCIPLES

Now Jesus begins to gather disciples about Him. Notice the following verses.

> **And Jesus, walking by the sea of Galilee, saw two brethren, Simon called Peter, and Andrew his brother, casting a net into the sea: for they were fishers.**
>
> **And he saith unto them, Follow me, and I will make you fishers of men [Matt. 4:18–19].**

In the Gospels the Lord makes at least three calls to these men, or perhaps it would be more accurate to say that three meetings took place between Christ and these men. The first meeting took place in Jerusalem, as recorded in John 1:35–42. Their second meeting took place by the Sea of Galilee, and apparently this is the record of it. They had seen Him before this, but at that time He had not called them to be with Him. Now here at the Sea of Galilee when He meets them again, He calls them to follow Him. And then we will find that they went back to fishing—Mark and Luke give us that detail. And finally He called them again, and that was to apostleship.

The wonder of it all is that Jesus called men like this. I have always felt that since He called imperfect men like the disciples were, He may be able to use me, and He may be able to use you. It is encouraging to know that we don't have to be super-duper saints to be used by Him. He may not make you a fisher of men, if you are not in the fishing business. But whatever business you are engaged in, He can use you. Whatever your talent may be, if you will turn it over to Him, He can use it. Years ago a lady in my church was absolutely tongue-tied when it came to witnessing for Christ, but she could bake the most marvelous cakes! She used to deplore the fact of her inability to witness, and I said to her one day, "Did it ever occur to you that the Lord may want you in the church family to bake cakes?" That may seem ridiculous, but it is not. The important thing for us is to give ourselves to Him. Under His direction He won't have us all doing the same thing because He gives us separate gifts. The body of Christ has many members in it, and they all have different functions to perform.

And they straightway left their nets, and followed him.

And going on from thence, he saw other two brethren, James the son of Zebedee, and John his brother, in a ship with Zebedee their father, mending their nets; and he called them.

And they immediately left the ship and their father, and followed him [Matt. 4:20–22].

These are very interesting men, and we will get better acquainted with them as we move along, especially as we see them in the other Gospel records.

Now remember that Jesus is in the northern section of Israel at this time—

And Jesus went about all Galilee, teaching in their synagogues, and preaching the gospel of the kingdom, and healing all manner of sickness and all manner of disease among the people [Matt. 4:23].

Notice that Jesus is *teaching* in their synagogues, and He is *preaching* the gospel of the Kingdom. What is it? The gospel (good news) of the Kingdom is that it is at hand in the person of the King. They are to accept and receive Him. Also, He is healing their physical illnesses. Friend, there were thousands of people in that day whom Jesus healed. Matthew especially lets us know that. If we will pay attention to the text, we will find that there were not just a few isolated cases, but thousands of folk were healed. That is the reason the enemies of Jesus never questioned His miracles—there were too many of them walking around. By the way, I live in Southern California where many so-called faith healers claim the healing of thousands of people, but we don't see these purported miracles walking around, at least they don't come my way.

And his fame went throughout all Syria: and they brought unto him all sick people that were taken with divers diseases and torments, and those which were possessed with devils, and those which were lunatic, and those that had the palsy; and he healed them [Matt. 4:24].

Notice the multitudes.

And there followed him great multitudes of people from Galilee, and from Decapolis, and from Jerusalem, and from Judaea, and from beyond Jordan [Matt. 4:25].

Decapolis was a district containing ten cities in the northeastern part of Galilee, east of the Jordan River. (I have had the privilege of visiting one of those cities.) Also, folk came up from Jerusalem and from Judea, the southernmost division of Palestine, and from beyond Jordan, which means a long way off. Jesus is ministering there in the north of Palestine.

It should be kept in mind as we consider the Gospel of Matthew that Matthew is making no attempt to give us a chronological record of the life of Christ. He is presenting Jesus in his Gospel as King, and he follows a pattern which is a movement in bringing the King and His claims to the nation Israel. This is important to observe. If we miss the movement in Matthew, we miss the purpose of this Gospel.

CHAPTER 5

THEME: The beginning of the so-called Sermon on the Mount dealing with the relationship of the subjects of the Kingdom to self and to law

INTRODUCTION TO THE SERMON ON THE MOUNT

Although we will consider each chapter of the Sermon on the Mount separately, let's first consider it as a whole. The Lord Jesus gave four major discourses. Matthew records three of them: (1) the Sermon on the Mount, chapters 5—7; (2) the Mystery Parables Discourse, chapter 13; and (3) the Olivet Discourse, chapters 24—25. The Sermon on the Mount is the manifesto of the King. The Mystery Parables Discourse gives the direction that the Kingdom of Heaven will take after Christ's rejection. The Olivet Discourse is prophetic, looking toward the future. There is a fourth discourse, recorded in John's Gospel, which deals with new truths and relationships in view of Christ's death, resurrection, ascension, and intercession. You and I are vitally connected with this latter discourse, by the way.

While the Sermon on the Mount is in Matthew 5—7, excerpts of it are in the other Gospels, also. It is unlikely that our Lord gave it only one time. He repeated, as you know, a great deal of the truths that He gave and probably gave this message, which we call the Sermon on the Mount, on many occasions. Luke records only a portion of it and mentions the fact that our Lord came down and stood on the plain, indicating that this was a different occasion. Frankly, Matthew's account is probably only a part of the Sermon on the Mount. I believe that our Lord gave a great deal more than we have here. However, this was given for our learning and our understanding today.

There are two things I would like to say by way of introduction to this section. One is that the far right and the far left are not confined to politics, but among theologians who expound Scripture we also have the far left and the far right. This is vividly revealed in the understanding of the Sermon on the Mount. The liberal theologian is to the far left. He treats the Sermon on the Mount as the gospel, the good news. He acts (even if he doesn't say it) as if it were the only important part of Scripture.

Many years ago I played handball with a very liberal preacher who later became rather famous as a leader of the liberal wing. One day he told me that all he needed of the Bible was the Sermon on the Mount. He went even so far as to say that all he needed was the Golden Rule, as recorded in Matthew 7:12: "Therefore all things whatsoever ye would that men should do to you, do ye even so to them: for this is the law and the prophets." To say that this is all the Bible you need may sound good, but it is pious drivel. The question is not whether you feel that the Sermon on the Mount is your religion. The question is: Are you *living* it? That is the important thing, and we'll have more to say about that later.

Those who reduce the Christian message to the Sermon on the Mount represent a very large segment of liberalism in our day. But please notice that the content of the Christian gospel is not found in the Sermon on the Mount. For instance, there is absolutely no mention of the death and resurrection of Christ. Yet Paul said to the Corinthians, ". . . I declare unto you the *gospel*. . . ." What is the gospel? The Sermon on the Mount? No. Paul made it clear that the gospel is this: ". . . that Christ died for our sins according to the scriptures; And that he was buried, and that he rose again the third day according to the scriptures" (1 Cor. 15:1, 3–4, italics mine). My friend, the gospel is not in the Sermon on the Mount, and that is the reason a great many people like to claim it as their religion. The preaching of that doctrine has made more hypocrites in the church than anything else. It is nothing in the world but verbiage for men to say, "I live by the Sermon on the Mount." If a man is honest and will *read* the Sermon on the Mount, he will *know* that he is not living up to it.

My friend, if the Sermon on the Mount is God's standard (and it is) and you come short of it, what are you going to do? Do you have a Savior who can extend mercy to you? Do you know the One who can reach down in grace and save you when you put your faith in Him?

To reduce the Christian message to the Sermon on the Mount is a simplicity which the Scriptures would not permit under any circumstances whatsoever. To do so is the extreme left point of view.

There is also the extreme right point of view. This group treats the Sermon on the Mount as if it were the bubonic plague. They have nothing to do with it. They give the impression that there is something ethically wrong with it. This group is known as hyper-dispensationalists. (Don't misunderstand, I am a dispensationalist but not a hyper-dispensationalist.) They maintain that we can't use the Sermon on the Mount at all. In fact, one of them told me that the Lord's Prayer has no meaning for us today. He was a prominent man, and after I heard him make that statement, I ran a sermon series on the Sermon on the Mount and the Lord's Prayer. In fact, I have a book entitled *Let Us Pray* which deals with the Lord's Prayer. The Lord's Prayer does have meaning for us in our day. It is *for* us although it is not *to* us. But the extreme right want to rule it out entirely.

It is true that there is no gospel in the Sermon on the Mount, and it is tragic indeed to give it to unregenerate man as a standard of conduct, and to tell him that if he tries to measure up to it, he is a Christian.

The Sermon on the Mount is Law lifted to the nth degree. Man could not keep the Law in the Old Testament. So how in the world can he keep, in his own strength, the Sermon on the Mount which is elevated to an even higher degree?

It is likewise true that the modus operandi for Christian living is not really found in the Sermon on the Mount. It gives the ethic without supplying the dynamic. Living by the power of the indwelling Holy Spirit is just not one of the truths taught in the Sermon on the Mount. Paul says: "For what the law could not do, in that it was weak through the flesh, God sending his own Son in the likeness of sinful flesh, and for sin, condemned sin in the flesh: That the righteousness of the law might be fulfilled in us, who walk not after the flesh, but after the Spirit" (Rom. 8:3–4).

You don't find that teaching in the Sermon on the Mount. It contains nothing of the ministry of the Holy Spirit. However, it does contain high ethical standards and practices which are not contrary to

Christian living; in fact, it expresses the mind of Christ which should be the mind of the Christian also. The great principles set down here are profitable for the Christian to study and learn, but he can never attain them in his own strength; he must go elsewhere to look for the *power*. What you have in the Sermon on the Mount is a marvelous electric light bulb, but you do not have the generator that produces the power that will make the light. And it is the light, not the bulb, that is all important.

The primary purpose of the Sermon on the Mount is to set before men the law of the Kingdom. In Matthew we are talking about the King who has come to present Himself. John the Baptist was His forerunner, and the King called disciples to follow Him. Now He enunciates the law of the Kingdom. This is the manifesto of the King and the platform of the Prince of Peace. And it's law! It will be the law of this world during the Millennium, and then it will find full fruition. Christ will reign on earth in person and will enforce every word of it. The Sermon on the Mount will finally prevail when He whose right it is to rule shall come. Now it's inconceivable to me that anyone who acknowledges Him today as Lord would despise this document or turn from it. The Christian who calls Jesus Christ *Lord*, will seek to do what He commands, but he can obey only in the power of the Holy Spirit. It is worse than futile to try to force the Sermon on the Mount on a gainsaying and rebellious world. Only the gospel of the grace of God can make men obedient to Christ, and it was given to bring men into *obedience* to God.

The Sermon on the Mount needs to be preached to bring conviction to the hearts of men. This document lets men know that they have sinned, and it reveals that none are righteous and that all have come short of God's glory.

The Christian can take the principles set down in the Sermon on the Mount and consider them in the light of other Scriptures. This will provide a wider view and a better understanding of the mind of Christ. For example, only here can you find Christ's definition of murder and adultery. Christ took two of the commandments and lifted them to the nth degree, "Thou shalt not kill" and "Thou shalt not commit adultery" (Exod. 20:13–14). Are these the only two which He lifted to a higher level? The answer seems to be obvious. These are the only two which are recorded in Matthew. Apparently, He did or could lift each commandment to a much higher level of attainment. If it could be said of the Mosaic Law, ". . . for by the works of the law shall no flesh be justified" (Gal. 2:16), then it would be ten times more difficult for a man to be justified by the Sermon on the Mount.

Try putting down upon your own life these two commandments: "Thou shalt not kill" and "Thou shalt not commit adultery." Let me illustrate what I mean by a little story. This incident took place during my first pastorate when I was a lot more blunt than I am now. An elder in the church I served in Nashville, Tennessee, invited me to speak at a Chamber of Commerce luncheon. This elder was a very wonderful man. He was the vice-president of a bank in the city, a member of the Chamber of Commerce, and when he asked me to bring a brief message, he said, "You won't have but a few minutes, but I want you to give these businessmen the gospel." Well, I arrived at the place a little early, and there were several men standing around. I went up near the speaker's table, and there was a man there who shook hands with me and began to rip out oaths. I had never seen such a fine-looking, well-dressed man curse as this man did. Finally, he said to me, "What's your racket?" I told him that I was a preacher, and he began to cover up immediately. He apologized for his language. He didn't need to apologize to me; he needed to apologize to God because God heard him all the time—which I told him. Then he wanted me to know that he was an officer in a certain liberal church, and he boasted, "The Sermon on the Mount is my religion."

"It is?" I said, "Let's shake hands. I congratulate you—you've got a wonderful religion! By the way, how are you doing with it?"

"What do you mean?"

"You said that the Sermon on the Mount is your religion. Are you living by it?"

"Well I try."

"That's not quite it. The Lord said that you are blessed if you do those things, not if you vote for them. Are you keeping it?"

"I think I am."

"Do you mind if we take a little test?"

"All right."

"The Sermon on the Mount says that if you are angry with your brother you are guilty of murder. Are you keeping that one?"

"Well, that's pretty strong, but I don't think I have been angry enough to kill anyone."

Then I quoted the one the Lord gave on adultery: "Whosoever looketh on a woman to lust after her hath committed adultery with her already in his heart" (v. 28), and asked him, "How about that one?"

"Oh, I guess that would get me."

"Well, I imagine that there are several things in the Sermon on the Mount that would get you. Apparently you are not living by your religion. If I were you, I'd change my religion and get something that works."

Oh, how many people there are like that man! They very piously say that the Sermon on the Mount is their religion, but all they mean is that they think it is a good document and a very fine expression, but it doesn't affect them one whit. I found out later that the man I was talking with had two wives—one at home and one at his office. My friend, if the Sermon on the Mount is your religion, you had better make sure you are keeping it. It is loaded with law. But if you will look at the Sermon on the Mount honestly, it will bring you to a Savior who died for you on the cross. The Sermon on the Mount sets before us great principles and high goals. We need to know them, but they reveal how far we come short.

Matthew's record of the Sermon on the Mount is, I am sure, only a skeleton of Christ's actual message. I have divided it like this:

1. Relationship of the subjects of the Kingdom to self (Matt. 5:1–16).
2. Relationship of the subjects of the Kingdom to law (Matt. 5:17–18).
3. Relationship of the subjects of the Kingdom to God (Matt. 6).
4. Relationship of the subjects of the Kingdom to others (Matt. 7).

The Sermon on the Mount opens with the Beatitudes. It is well to note that they are be-attitudes, not do-attitudes. They state what the subjects of the Kingdom are—they are the type of person described in the Beatitudes.

Verse 1 makes it clear why this discourse is called the Sermon on the Mount.

First it should be noted that the Lord did not actually give the Sermon on the Mount to the multitudes. He gave it to His disciples, those who were already His.

RELATIONSHIP OF THE SUBJECTS OF THE KINGDOM TO SELF

And seeing the multitudes, he went up into a mountain: and when he was set, his disciples came unto him:

And he opened his mouth, and taught them, saying [Matt. 5:1–2].

Although He did not actually give the Sermon on the Mount to the multitudes, He gave it to the disciples because He saw the multitudes and their need. Therefore, it was given to the multitudes indirectly.

In our day, men need first to come to Christ. While the Kingdom is actually in abeyance, the present state of it is a place where the seed is being sown, and the seed is the Word of God. Our business in the world is to sow the seed, and the day is coming when Christ will establish His Kingdom upon this earth.

Blessed are the poor in spirit: for theirs is the kingdom of heaven [Matt. 5:3].

This verse says, "Blessed are the poor in spirit." It doesn't tell you *how* to become poor in spirit; it just says, "Blessed are the poor in spirit." In these twelve verses, our Lord used the word *blessed* nine times. By the way, the Psalms open with the same word: "Blessed is the man . . ." (Ps. 1:1). This is in contrast to the curses of the Mosaic Law. You may remember that Joshua was told that when the people of Israel were come over Jordan, they were to stand on Mount Gerizim to bless the people. And then the curses were to be given from Mount Ebal. The blessings from the Sermon on the Mount are in sharp contrast to the curses from Mount Ebal, and they far exceed the blessings from Mount Gerizim, because Christ alone can bring those blessings. In our day only the saved sinner can know his poverty of spirit— "Blessed are the poor in spirit." The Sermon on the Mount, instead of making folk poor in spirit, makes them boast—like the man I referred to. He was boasting that the Sermon on the Mount was his religion, and he was trying to kid himself and kid me into thinking that he was keeping it. He wasn't keeping it at all; it was just making a hypocrite out of him. And there are a lot of those around.

I played golf one day in Tulsa, Oklahoma, with a very wealthy oil man. He told me, "I went to church just like the rest of the hypocrites, and I was one of them, talking about keeping the Sermon on the Mount. Then one day I found out that I was a lost sinner on the way to hell. I turned to Jesus Christ, and He saved me!" Oh, my friend, don't be deceived. Only the Spirit of God can reveal to you your poverty of spirit. The Lord Jesus in the Sermon on the Mount was not telling His disciples *how* to become citizens of the Kingdom of Heaven. They already were citizens of the Kingdom.

We Christians today are actually very poor in spirit, we are spiritually bankrupt, but we have something to give which is more valuable than silver and gold. Paul expressed it this way: 'As sorrowful, yet alway rejoicing; as poor, yet making many rich; as having nothing, and yet possessing all things" (2 Cor. 6:10). "As poor, yet making many rich" is referring to spiritual riches which are available to everyone who belongs to Christ.

The next beatitude is:

Blessed are they that mourn: for they shall be comforted [Matt. 5:4].

It is interesting to note that the same thoughts expressed in the Beatitudes can be found elsewhere in the Scriptures. The poor in spirit are referred to in Zephaniah 3:12. Micah is an example of those who mourn and are comforted (see ch. 7).

Blessed are the meek: for they shall inherit the earth [Matt. 5:5].

We find this in Psalm 37:11. The meek are not inheriting the earth in this day in which we live—I'm sure you recognize that. So apparently the Sermon on the Mount is not in effect today. However, when Christ is reigning, the meek will inherit the earth.

How do you become meek? Our Lord was meek and lowly, and He will inherit all things; we are the heirs of God and joint-heirs with Jesus Christ. We are told that the fruit of the Spirit is love, joy, peace, long-suffering, gentleness, goodness, faith, temperance, and meekness. Only the Spirit of God can break you and make you meek. If you could produce meekness by your own effort, you would be proud of yourself, wouldn't you? And out goes your meekness! Meekness is not produced by self-effort but by Spirit effort. Only the Holy Spirit can produce meekness in the heart of a yielded Christian. The Christian who has learned the secret of producing the fruit of the Holy Spirit can turn here to the Beatitudes and read, "Blessed are the meek: for they shall inherit the earth," and see that the rewards of meekness are still in the future. Paul asked the Corinthian believers, "Do ye not know that the saints shall judge the world? . . ." (1 Cor. 6:2).

The Beatitudes present goals which the child of God wants to realize in his own life, but he can't do it on his own. You may have heard of the preacher who had a message entitled "Meekness and How I Attained It." He said that he hadn't delivered his message yet, but as soon as he got an audience big enough, he was going to give it! Well, I have a notion that he had long since lost his meekness. Meekness can only be a fruit of the Holy Spirit.

Then in verse six we are told:

Blessed are they which do hunger and thirst after righteousness: for they shall be filled [Matt. 5:6].

What about the natural man; does he hunger and thirst for righteousness? The ones I meet do not! "But the natural man receiveth not the things of the Spirit of God: for they are foolishness unto him: neither can he know them, because they are spiritually discerned" (1 Cor. 2:14). The "natural man" is in contrast to the spiritual man who has found that Christ is his righteousness—". . . of him are ye in Christ

Jesus, who of God is made unto us wisdom, and righteousness, and sanctification, and redemption" (1 Cor. 1:30).

Blessed are the merciful: for they shall obtain mercy [Matt. 5:7].

This beatitude is so misunderstood in our day because it makes our obtaining mercy conditional on our being merciful. This is not the condition on which *we* obtain mercy—"Not by works of righteousness which we have done, but according to his *mercy* he saved us, by the washing of regeneration, and renewing of the Holy Ghost" (Titus 3:5, italics mine). We should be merciful *because* we have obtained mercy. "But ye are a chosen generation, a royal priesthood, an holy nation, a peculiar people; that ye should shew forth the praises of him who hath called you out of darkness into his marvelous light: Which in time past were not a people, but are now the people of God: which had not obtained mercy, but now have obtained mercy" (1 Pet. 2:9-10).

Blessed are the pure in heart: for they shall see God [Matt. 5:8].

No honest man can say that his heart is pure. How can the heart of man, which is desperately wicked, be made clean? The Lord Jesus said, "Now ye are clean through the word which I have spoken unto you" (John 15:3). It is by the washing of regeneration that we are made clean. Only the blood of Christ can cleanse us from all sin (see 1 John 1:7).

Blessed are the peacemakers: for they shall be called the children of God [Matt. 5:9].

Can you name one peacemaker in the world right now? There is no one today who can make peace. Christ alone is the great Peacemaker. He made peace by His blood between a righteous God and an unrighteous sinner. "Therefore being justified by faith, we have peace with God through our Lord Jesus Christ" (Rom. 5:1).

> **Blessed are they which are persecuted for righteousness' sake: for theirs is the kingdom of heaven [Matt. 5:10].**

The application of this beatitude to our day and to the remnant of Israel during the Great Tribulation is easy to see. But can it apply to the Kingdom which is to be established? Won't all evil be removed in the Kingdom? Well, many Scriptures show that in the millennial Kingdom there will still be evil in the world because it will be a time of testing. The outbreak of rebellion at the end of the Millennium reveals that evil will be prevalent during the Millennium (see Rev. 20:7–9).

> **Ye are the salt of the earth: but if the salt have lost his savour, wherewith shall it be salted? it is thenceforth good for nothing, but to be cast out, and to be trodden under foot of men.**

> **Ye are the light of the world. A city that is set on an hill cannot be hid [Matt. 5:13–14].**

God's people in any age and under any condition are both salt and light in the world. The Scots translate "savour" by the more expressive word *tang*. I like their word much better. "If the salt has lost its tang." The problem today is that most church members have not only lost their tang as salt, but as pepper they have lost their pep also. We have very few salt and pepper Christians in our day. Now salt doesn't keep fermentation and that type of thing from taking place, but it will arrest it. You and I ought to be the salt in the earth and have an influence for good in the world.

Christians are also the light of the world. Certainly in the Kingdom the believers are going to be the light of the world. This is a tremendous principle for us. We need to be a light in our neighborhood and wherever we go. We have no light within ourselves, but the Word of God is light. Being a light means giving out the Word of God in one way or another. This doesn't mean that you should be quoting Scripture all the time, but it does mean that you are to share the light that

God has given you. It is very easy to cultivate some person, then quietly and graciously introduce them to a Bible-teaching church or radio program. There are many ways in which you can be light in the world.

Let your light so shine before men, that they may see your good works, and glorify your Father which is in heaven [Matt. 5:16].

There are those of the liberal persuasion that feel the Sermon on the Mount is anthropocentric, or man-centered, rather than theocentric, or God-centered. (Those are their terms.) But, obviously, the Sermon on the Mount is *not* anthropocentric, man-centered. It is theocentric. Does this verse say, "Let your light so shine before men, that they may see your good works, and glorify *you* and pat you on the back, and give you a gold medal and a loving cup?" No! This verse says that you and I are to let our light so shine in this world that we may glorify our Father which is in heaven. The Sermon on the Mount is God-centered. During the Millennium, during the Kingdom here on earth, everything which is done and said will be God-centered. And in the present age, in this lost world in which you and I live today, our prime motivation should be to bring glory to God. This is something that every Christian should consider very seriously. The aim and purpose of our lives should be to glorify our God.

RELATIONSHIP OF THE SUBJECTS OF THE KINGDOM TO LAW

Think not that I am come to destroy the law, or the prophets: I am not come to destroy, but to fulfil [Matt. 5:17].

Remember that part of the Mosaic Law was the ceremonial law. Christ was the sacrifice for the sins of the world, the Lamb slain before the foundation of the earth. Christ came not to destroy the Law but to fulfill the Law. He fulfilled it in that He kept it during His earthly life. And the standard which was set before man *He* was able to attain, and now He is able to make over to you and me (and every believer) His own righteousness. God's standards have not changed, but you and I cannot attain them in our own strength. We need help; we need a Savior. We do need mercy, and we obtain mercy when we come to Christ.

> **For verily I say unto you, Till heaven and earth pass, one jot or one tittle shall in no wise pass from the law, till all be fulfilled [Matt. 5:18].**

I hope you don't misinterpret what I am saying in this section which we call the Sermon on the Mount. I am not saying that we are free to break the Mosaic Law. The fact of the matter is that the Law is still a standard. It reveals to me that I cannot measure up to God's standard. This drives me to the Cross of Christ. The only way I can fulfill the Law is by accepting the only One who could fulfill it—Jesus Christ.

> **Whosoever therefore shall break one of these least commandments, and shall teach men so, he shall be called the least in the kingdom of heaven: but whosoever shall do and teach them, the same shall be called great in the kingdom of heaven [Matt. 5:19].**

You cannot break the commandments and get by with it. But you cannot keep them in your own strength. The only way you can keep them is to come to Jesus Christ for salvation, power, and strength. The commandments are not a *way* of salvation but a *means* to show you the way to salvation through the acceptance of the work of Jesus Christ.

> **For I say unto you, That except your righteousness shall exceed the righteousness of the scribes and Pharisees, ye shall in no case enter into the kingdom of heaven [Matt. 5:20].**

It is very important to see His point right here. The Pharisees had a high degree of righteousness according to the Law, but that was not acceptable. How can you and I surpass their righteousness? It is impossible in our own efforts. We need Christ to do it for us.

> **Ye have heard that it was said by them of old time, Thou shalt not kill; and whosoever shall kill shall be in danger of the judgment:**
>
> **But I say unto you, That whosoever is angry with his brother without a cause shall be in danger of the judgment: and whosoever shall say to his brother, Raca, shall be in danger of the council: but whosoever shall say, Thou fool, shall be in danger of hell fire [Matt. 5:21–22].**

This is a tremendous statement! It means that if you are angry with your brother, you are a murderer! Do you claim to be keeping the Mosaic Law? You cannot break the Law and get by with it. You can't get by with mouthing the boast that the Sermon on the Mount is your religion and then break every part of it. My friend, both you and I need a Savior who has perfectly kept the Law and can impute to us His own righteousness.

> **Verily I say unto thee, Thou shalt by no means come out thence, till thou hast paid the uttermost farthing [Matt. 5:26].**

Note that Jesus says, "Verily I say unto thee." He is lifting His teaching above the teaching of Moses. He is lifting Himself to the position of the Lawgiver and also the Interpreter, by the way.

> **Ye have heard that it was said by them of old time, Thou shalt not commit adultery:**
>
> **But I say unto you, That whosoever looketh on a woman to lust after her hath committed adultery with her already in his heart [Matt. 5:27–28].**

For many years I have publicly made the statement that nobody but the Lord Jesus has ever kept the Law. One Sunday morning I repeated it in my message, and afterward a big, burly, red-faced fellow came to me and said, "You always say that nobody keeps the Law. I want you to know that *I* keep the Law!" By the way, he belonged to a cult although he attended services at the church I pastored. Since he claimed to keep the Law, I said, "All right, let's look at it," and I showed him verse 22 regarding hatred being the same as murder. He said that he kept that, although I don't believe that he did. So I gave him verse 28 and said, "It says here that if you so much as look upon a woman to lust after her, you have committed adultery. Now look me straight in the eye and tell me that you have never done that." He was red-faced to begin with, but you should have seen him then—he was really red-faced. He grunted some sort of epithet, turned on his heels, and walked out. Of course, he walked out! And I say to you, if you are honest, you will not claim to be keeping the Law. Remember that there were ten commandments. Although Matthew mentions only these two that Christ dealt with, I am of the opinion that He lifted all ten of them to the nth degree.

Oh, my friend, the Sermon on the Mount shows me that I have sinned and that I need to come to Him for mercy and help. To say that you are living by the Sermon on the Mount while all the time you are breaking it is to declare that the Law is not important.

In the following verses the Lord deals in a tremendous way with the Law and man's relationship to it.

And if thy right eye offend thee, pluck it out, and cast it from thee: for it is profitable for thee that one of thy members should perish, and not that thy whole body should be cast into hell.

And if thy right hand offend thee, cut it off, and cast it from thee: for it is profitable for thee that one of thy members should perish, and not that thy whole body should be cast into hell [Matt. 5:29–30].

This is severe, very severe, and it reveals, friends, that if you cannot meet God's standards, you need a Savior. Don't kid yourself and fool around with pretending that you are keeping the Law. You are only being a hypocrite. In Christian circles we are intent upon patting each other on the back and complimenting one another and giving each other credit for what we do when all the time we all are a pack of low-down, dirty, rotten sinners, not even fit for heaven. The Sermon on the Mount ought to drive you to the Cross of Christ where you cry out for mercy. To do that is to honor the Law, my friend. Don't try to kid me into thinking that you are keeping it. I know you're not—because you are just like I am.

> It hath been said, Whosoever shall put away his wife, let him give her a writing of divorcement:
>
> But I say onto you, That whosoever shall put away his wife, saving for the cause of fornication, causeth her to commit adultery: and whosoever shall marry her that is divorced committeth adultery [Matt. 5:31–32].

Here the Lord gives the grounds for divorce. If someone is divorced for a reason not given in Scripture, that person is an adulterer. This is something that is entirely ignored today in Christian circles. This, however, will be the Law during the Kingdom age because there will be men and women who will want to leave their mates during that period. We will deal with the divorce question in some detail when we get to chapter 19.

> Again, ye have heard that it hath been said by them of old time, Thou shalt not forswear thyself, but shalt perform onto the Lord thine oaths:
>
> But I say unto you, Swear not at all; neither by heaven; for it is God's throne:
>
> Nor by the earth; for it is his footstool: neither by Jerusalem; for it is the city of the great King [Matt. 5:33–35].

The Lord Jesus is saying that we are to be the kind of persons who don't have to take an oath. As a boy, I can remember that my dad could go into the bank and borrow money, then come back a couple of days later to sign the note. Or he could call the bank by phone and have a certain amount of money credited to his account. Well, believe me, it is different in our day. Why? Because there are a lot more folk today who cannot be trusted. The Lord says that the child of God, under all circumstances, should be trustworthy. The Lord says:

> **But let your communication be, Yea, yea; Nay, nay: for whatsoever is more than these cometh of evil [Matt. 5:37].**

When a man says to me, "I'd swear on a stack of Bibles a mile high," that is the fellow I do not believe because I think the lie he's telling is a mile high.

> **Ye have heard that it hath been said, An eye for an eye, and a tooth for a tooth [Matt. 5:38].**

All of that will be changed when Christ is reigning in His Kingdom.

> **But I say unto you, That ye resist not evil: but whosoever shall smite thee on thy right cheek, turn to him the other also [Matt. 5:39].**

Do you live like this, or do you resist evil? There is a principle for us here, but we are living in a day when a wise man armed keepeth his house. And Paul could say, "Alexander the coppersmith did me much evil: the Lord reward him according to his works" (2 Tim. 4:14). In the Kingdom you will be able to turn the other cheek. It reminds me of the Irishman whom someone hit on the cheek and knocked down. The Irishman got up and turned his other cheek. The fellow knocked him down again. This time the Irishman got up and beat the stuffin' out of that fellow. An observer asked, "Why did you do that?" "Well," replied the Irishman, "the Lord said to turn the other cheek and I did, but He never told me what to do after that."

And if any man will sue thee at the law, and take away thy coat, let him have thy cloak also.

And whosoever shall compel thee to go a mile, go with him twain.

Give to him that asketh thee, and from him that would borrow of thee turn not thou away [Matt. 5:40–42].

If you have a banker who says that he is living by the Sermon on the Mount, give this verse to him and see how far you get with it. Let's quit being hypocrites and realize that this is the law of the Kingdom. When my Lord is on the throne down here on this earth, folk can live this way. In our day, business could not be conducted by this law. Years ago Archbishop McGee of Ireland said that it was impossible to conduct the affairs of the British nation on the basis of the Sermon on the Mount. I do not know whether I am related to Archbishop McGee or not, but I certainly find that I *think* as he did about the Sermon on the Mount. Although it contains great principles for the Christian in our day, it can be enforced only when Christ is on the throne. I think that ought to be quite obvious.

In our contemporary society many of the wealthy churches say that they follow the Sermon on the Mount. That is what the congregation gets as a steady diet on Sunday morning. However, if you go to the rich and try to get something from them, you won't get very far, I assure you. On Sunday they hear, "Give to him that asketh thee, and from him that would borrow of thee turn not thou away." It sounds great. They think the Sermon on the Mount is a great document, but on Monday morning it is cold-blooded business and cash on the barrelhead. That, of course, is the way the business world is set up today.

However, there is a great principle in these verses for us, and we should not miss that. Certainly we should be helpful to those who are in need. And there are many fine Christian acts that can be performed by believers. Historically, hospitals, orphan homes, and works of charity (which the Bible calls acts of love) have followed the preaching of the gospel. I do not know any place on earth where they preceded the gospel, but they always followed it. There should be the fruit of good works in a believer's life.

> **Ye have heard that it hath been said, Thou shalt love thy neighbour, and hate thine enemy.**
>
> **But I say unto you, Love your enemies, bless them that curse you, do good to them that hate you, and pray for them which despitefully use you, and persecute you [Matt. 5:43–44].**

This rule, I insist, is for the Kingdom. The Lord Jesus lifts the Mosaic Law to the nth degree. He says that in the Kingdom the enemy is to be loved instead of hated.

The believer today operates on a different principle. We are commanded to love all believers, and we express our love to our enemies by getting the gospel to them, giving them the message of God's saving grace that is able to bring them to heaven.

In concluding this chapter, our Lord says that we are to be perfect—

> **Be ye therefore perfect, even as your Father which is in heaven is perfect [Matt. 5:48].**

How is it possible for you and me to be perfect? We are accepted in Christ, in the beloved.

There is no condemnation to them which are in Christ, and we get in Christ by faith in Him. The only way we can become perfect is through our faith in Christ—Christ imputes to us His righteousness. And then begins the slow process of sanctification in which God attempts to conform us to the image of His Son. This, of course, should be the goal of every believer. But seeking to attain perfection by our own efforts is absolutely futile. Do you think that you can go to God and say, "Look what I have done: look how wonderful I am," trying to get all the glory for yourself and to force God to save you on that basis?

My friend, you are going to do nothing of the kind because you and I are not perfect. Most of us remember this:

> Little Jack Horner
> Sat in a corner
> Eating a Christmas pie;
> He put in his thumb,
> And pulled out a plum,
> And said, What a good boy am I!

We see a lot of that in religion today. Little folk sit around, reach in their thumb, and pull out a plum and say, "What a good boy am I!" My friend, you and I are not good by God's standards. We need a Savior.

As we have seen, in this chapter the King speaks of the righteousness which His subjects must possess. And it must be a righteousness to exceed the righteousness of the scribes and Pharisees. They had a religious righteousness. For instance, Nicodemus was an outstanding man, and he was religious. You can't find much to criticize about him. But our Lord said to him, "You have to be born again" (see John 3:1–8). Now we have to have a righteousness superior to that of the scribes and the Pharisees, and it can only come through trust in Christ.

CHAPTER 6

THEME: The inner motives which govern external acts of righteousness, such as the giving of alms, prayer, fasting, and the getting of riches; the relationship of the subjects of the Kingdom of Heaven to God

THE MOTIVE AND METHOD OF GIVING ALMS

Chapter 6 of Matthew deals with the external part of religion. We have seen in chapter 5 that the King speaks of the righteousness which His subjects must possess. It must be a righteousness to exceed the righteousness of the scribes and Pharisees, and that comes only through trust in Christ. In chapter 6 Matthew talks about the righteousness that the subjects of the Kingdom are to *practice*. The motive, of course, is the important thing in what you do for God. No third party can enter into this relationship. These things are between the soul and God.

The items mentioned in this chapter—the giving of alms, prayer, fasting, money, and taking thought and care for the future—are very practical considerations.

First, our Lord talks about alms. Keep in mind that all of this has to do with externalities of religion or with ostentation in religion.

Take heed that ye do not your alms before men, to be seen of them: otherwise ye have no reward of your Father which is in heaven [Matt. 6:1].

Although the Lord Jesus is directing His remarks to the subjects of His coming Kingdom, there is a great principle here for you and me.

Therefore when thou doest thine alms, do not sound a trumpet before thee, as the hypocrites do in the synagogues and in the streets, that they may have glory of men. Verily I say unto you, They have their reward [Matt. 6:2].

He is saying this with biting irony. Believe me, He knew how to use the rapier of sarcasm! When the Pharisees wanted to give something to the poor, it was their custom to go down to a busy street corner in Jerusalem and blow a trumpet. Although the purpose was to call the poor and needy together to receive the gifts, it afforded a fine opportunity to let others see their good works. Do you see parallels today in the way some Christians give? Our Lord said that when the Pharisees do it that way, they have their reward. What was their reward? Well, what was it that they were after? Jesus said they did it to have glory of men. They blew the trumpet, and everybody came running out to see how generously they gave, and that was their reward. Their giving was not between themselves and God.

Now, why do you give? There is more than one way to give. Several years ago I was asked to take an offering in a certain organization. I was told to be sure and give everybody an opportunity to stand up and tell how much he would give. For example, I was instructed to say, "How many will give one hundred dollars?" I asked, "Why in the world do you take an offering like that?" I was told that a certain man would attend who would give only one dollar if a regular offering was taken. However, if the question of how many would give one hundred dollars was asked, he would give that amount. May I say that he blew a trumpet. And I discovered when I came to know this man that this was the way he gave.

There are other people who give large checks but want to hand them to you personally. There was a man in my church who always gave me a check before I went into the pulpit. He thought this would excite me enough so that I would mention it. A friend of his came to me one day and said, "So-and-so is disturbed." He went on to explain that I did not acknowledge the very large check his friend had given me last Sunday. "That's right," I said, and told this man the reason why. "Your friend is a man of means and the check he gave me, in relationship to what he has, wasn't very much. Last Sunday a mail-carrier also handed me an envelope. He didn't want me to open it until after the service and did not want me to say a word to anyone about it. He gave me almost twice as much money as the man of means did. If I were going to acknowledge anybody, it would have to be the mail-carrier—but he didn't want me to do that."

May I say to you that giving is between you and God, and the very minute you get a third party involved, you don't get any credit in heaven.

There is a lot of so-called Christian giving today that isn't giving at all. For example, the college I graduated from played on human nature. While I was in school, beautiful architectural plans were drawn up for a tower to be put on an old hall. It was modestly announced that the tower would be named after the donor. At least a half dozen people wanted their names on that tower. Today it is called "So-and-so Tower" in honor of a certain man. His name is carved in stone which means that his trumpet is being blown all the time. A lot of people give like that. This kind of giving is worth nothing before God.

> **But when thou doest alms, let not thy left hand know what thy right hand doeth:**
>
> **That thine alms may be in secret: and thy Father which seeth in secret himself shall reward thee openly [Matt. 6:3–4].**

Don't reach in your pocket with one hand and then put the other hand in the air to let people know how much you are giving! Our Lord is saying that when you put your hand in your pocket to get something to give, be so secretive about it that the other hand doesn't know what you are doing. All of this is biting sarcasm.

Do our liberal friends really live by the Sermon on the Mount? I don't think they do!

THE MARKS OF GENUINE PRAYER

And when thou prayest, thou shalt not be as the hypocrites are: for they love to pray standing in the synagogues and in the corners of the streets, that they may be

seen of men. Verily I say unto you, They have their re-
ward [Matt. 6:5].

"Thou shalt not be as the *hypocrites* are"—my, our Lord used strong
language, didn't He! "They have their reward." They pray so that they
may be seen of men. A man might go wearing a prayer shawl, which
advertises the fact that he is praying. Jesus said that when a man prays
like that, he has his reward. He gets what he wants—that is, to be seen
of men. But his prayer never gets above the rafters of the building.

But thou, when thou prayest, enter into thy closet, and
when thou hast shut thy door, pray to thy Father which
is in secret; and thy Father which seeth in secret shall
reward thee openly [Matt. 6:6].

The concept we are dealing with here is revolutionary. Did you notice
that the Lord uses the term *Father*? These are citizens of the Kingdom that the Lord is talking about. How do you become a child of God
today? John 1:12 gives us the answer: "But as many as received him,
to them gave he power [the authority] to become the sons of God, even
to them that [do no more or less than] believe on his name." Our Lord
even said to Nicodemus, "You must be born again" (see John 3:3)—
until then, you can't call God your Father. And in the Old Testament
you will not find the word *Father* used in relation to a man with God.
The nation Israel as a whole was called by God, ". . . Israel is my
son . . ." (Exod. 4:22), but not an individual. The Lord Jesus is speaking of a new relationship.

Concerning the subject of prayer, we are told that it should be secret and sincere. Many an unknown saint of God will be revealed at
the judgment seat of Christ as a real person of prayer.

But when ye pray, use not vain repetitions, as the hea-
then do: for they think that they shall be heard for their
much speaking [Matt. 6:7].

I heard a fellow pray the other day, and he repeated his petition about a dozen times. The Lord Jesus says that if we ask the Father one time, He hears us.

> **Be not ye therefore like unto them: for your Father knoweth what things ye have need of, before ye ask him [Matt. 6:8].**

Prayer should be marked by sincerity and simplicity:
1. Sincerity—Matthew 6:6. Go in and close the door—your prayer is between you and God.
2. Simplicity—Matthew 6:7. Don't use vain repetition. Get right down to the nitty-gritty and tell the Lord what you have on your mind. "Your Father knoweth what things ye have need of, before ye ask him" v. 8. Even though He already knows what we need, He wants us to come to Him and ask.

Now He gives us a sample prayer—"After this manner therefore pray ye."

Before we look at this so-called Lord's Prayer, let me say that I never use it in a public service. I don't think that a Sunday morning crowd should get up and pray, "Give us this day our daily bread" when they have a roast in the oven at home—they already have their meal. It is a very meaningful prayer for those who are hungry, but a well-fed Sunday morning congregation ought not to pray this because for them it is vain repetition.

However, it is a wonderful model prayer for believers of all conditions.

> **After this manner therefore pray ye: Our Father which art in heaven, Hallowed by thy name [Matt. 6:9].**

Notice that this so-called Lord's Prayer could not be the prayer of the Lord Jesus. He couldn't pray this prayer. He couldn't join with you and me and say, "Our Father" because the relationship between the Father and the Son is the relationship in deity. It is a position, not a begetting. I became a son of God only through faith in Christ; therefore Christ couldn't join with me in saying, "Our Father."

"Which art in heaven." God is not a prisoner in this universe—He is beyond and above it. He is in the air spaces, in the stellar spaces, but He is far removed from His universe today. He is more than creation! He is the One sitting upon the throne of the universe, and He has it under His control!

"Hallowed be thy name," more correctly translated, would read, "Let thy name be made holy." The name of God stands for God, for all that God is. In what way can you and I make God's name holy? It is my conviction that by our lives we are to make God's name holy. When Abraham went into Canaan, a Canaanite passing by observed that they had a new neighbor, for he had seen Abraham's altar. Everywhere Abraham went he built an altar to God. And when Abraham began to do business with the Canaanites, they found him to be honest. They found that everything Abraham said invited their confidence. Finally, they reached the conclusion that the God whom Abraham worshiped was a holy God, and Abimelech said to Abraham, ". . . God is with thee in all that thou doest" (Gen. 21:22). The children of Heth said, ". . . thou art a mighty prince among us . . ." (Gen. 23:6). The entire life of Abraham revealed the reverence he felt for God. Surely the name of God was made holy in Canaan because of Abraham.

Thy kingdom come. Thy will be done in earth, as it is in heaven [Matt. 6:10].

"Thy kingdom come" is the Kingdom about which Matthew has been speaking, the Kingdom which Christ will establish on this earth. This is a worthy petition for all of us to pray.

Give us this day our daily bread [Matt. 6:11].

As I have indicated, this prayer is a model for our own prayers. Now I want you to notice this petition for a moment. It is a wonderful petition, so simple yet one that should come from our hearts with great enthusiasm. It speaks of our utter dependence upon God. Our bodily wants, our physical necessities, all are supplied by Him day by day. "Give us . . . our daily bread"—just as Israel gathered manna for the day, they gathered nothing for the morrow. They were not permitted to gather manna for the next week. They could not hoard it. This prayer gathers manna every day, "Give us this *day* our daily bread." It shows man that he lives from hand to mouth. It shows man that even his bodily necessities, his basic needs, come from God.

And forgive us our debts, as we forgive our debtors [Matt. 6:12].

Our Lord Jesus could not pray this—He had no sin to be forgiven. You see, it is not the Lord's prayer; it is the disciples' prayer.

"Forgive us our debts as we forgive those that are indebted to us" is legalistic; it is not grace. I thank God for another verse of Scripture, Ephesians 4:32, "And be ye kind one to another, tenderhearted, forgiving one another, even as God for Christ's sake hath forgiven you." Today God is forgiving us on the basis of what Christ has done for us, not on the basis by which we forgive—as touching the matter of our salvation. The redemption of God is in full view when God forgives us. It does not refer to our salvation when we read, "forgive us our debts as we forgive our debtors." He is speaking here to those who are already saved, those who already have the nature of God. He does not wait for you to forgive before He forgives. This is not His method of settling the sin question. He gave His Son to die, and it is on this basis that God forgives.

In some churches today where there is formal religion, liturgy, and ritual, they use "forgive us our debts" while others will use "forgive us our trespasses." Two little girls were talking about the Lord's Prayer as repeated in their churches. One said, "We have trespasses in our church," and the other said, "Well, in our church we have debts." (Probably they both were right as far as the churches of our day are concerned—they have both debts and trespasses.) So which phrase is accurate? There is no difficulty here at all since all of these words refer to the same thing, and that thing is sin.

And lead us not into temptation, but deliver us from evil:
For thine is the kingdom, and the power, and the glory,
for ever. Amen [Matt. 6:13].

"Lead us not into temptation." This word *lead* gives us the wrong impression because James says God does not tempt any man. That is true—God does not tempt any man. A better translation here would be, "Leave us not in temptation." It does not mean to keep us out of it, but when we are in it, do not leave us there.

"Deliver us from evil"—this deliverance is from the evil one. Deliver us from the evil one—deliver us from the Devil. Satan is today an awful reality. The world has tried many times to get rid of him. They laughed at Martin Luther who threw an inkwell at him. But recently we have had a turn in events. Any man who stands for God knows the awful reality of Satan. As we work in any church we become conscious of the presence of God and also dreadfully conscious of the presence of Satan. But we have this petition, "Deliver us from the evil one."

May I say that this is a marvelous prayer for a new believer to pray privately in learning to pray. My own mother was not saved until late in life. She didn't know how to pray, and she began by just repeating the Lord's Prayer. Finally she graduated from this, and she could pray her own prayer.

When we are teaching our children to pray, we begin them with, "Now I lay me down to sleep." Then one day little Willie adds, "God bless Mama and God bless Papa." That is a thrilling moment for us, because they are beginning to pray on their own. And our Lord gave the so-called Lord's Prayer as a model. It is a glorious, wonderful prayer, and it shows us what we should include in our own prayers. He would like us to learn to pray in our own words when we talk to Him.

As the Lord Jesus said in the verses preceding the Lord's Prayer, prayer is not to be done for display. It is a relationship between you and God, and the most effective prayer is when you enter into your closet—that is, a private place. I am not enthusiastic about public prayer meetings because of the fact that the deadest service of any in the church is the prayer meeting. As a pastor, I used to try to build up the prayer meeting, but I soon discovered that if you have fifty dead saints praying, you don't improve it by getting a hundred dead saints. It still is a pretty dead prayer meeting. What we need is a great deal more *private* prayer. It should take place between an individual and God.

THE MEANING OF FASTING

The Lord moves on now to the subject of fasting.

> **Moreover when ye fast, be not, as the hypocrites, of a sad countenance: for they disfigure their faces, that they may appear unto men to fast. Verily I say unto you, They have their reward [Matt. 6:16].**

Fasting has a value for believers in our day, I am convinced of that, but only if it is done privately. It should be a personal matter between the soul and God.

> **But thou, when thou fastest, anoint thine head, and wash thy face;**
>
> **That thou appear not unto men to fast, but unto thy Father which is in secret: and thy Father, which seeth in secret, shall reward thee openly [Matt. 6:17–18].**

THE MAKING OF MONEY AND THE MEANING OF REAL RICHES

The Lord next turns to the subject of money. This is something many people don't like the preacher to talk about.

> **Lay not up for yourselves treasures upon earth, where moth and rust doth corrupt, and where thieves break through and steal:**

> But lay up for yourselves treasures in heaven, where
> neither moth nor rust doth corrupt, and where thieves
> do not break through nor steal:
>
> For where your treasure is, there will your heart be also
> [Matt. 6:19-21].

A great many folk think that money cannot be used in a spiritual way
and that when you talk about money, you are talking about something
that is only material. However, our Lord says that we are to lay up for
ourselves treasure in heaven. How can we do that? Well, instead of
putting it in a bank in Switzerland, put it in heaven by giving it to the
Lord's work down here—but make sure it is in the *Lord's* work. You
ought to investigate everything you give to. Make sure that you are
giving to that which will accumulate treasure for you in heaven. If it is
used for the propagation of the gospel and to get out the Word of God,
it becomes legal tender in heaven, and that is how we gather treasure
in heaven.

Perhaps you are saying, "But I don't give for *that* reason." You
ought to, because our Lord said, "Lay up for yourselves treasures in
heaven." That is a laudable motive for giving. And He gives the reason: "For where your treasure is, there will your heart be also." If you
get enough treasure laid up in heaven, you are certainly going to think
a lot about heaven. But if it is in the bank, your thoughts are going to
be on the bank. There is an ever-present danger of worshiping mam-
mon rather than God.

MATERIAL THINGS AND THE CHRISTIAN'S
RELATIONSHIP TO THEM

Matthew 6 concludes with our Lord talking about other things that
are material. He tells us that we are not to give much thought to our
material needs. For example, the Lord says:

> Behold the fowls of the air: for they sow not, neither do
> they reap, nor gather into barns; yet your heavenly

Father feedeth them. Are ye not much better than they?
[Matt. 6:26].

Birds cannot sow. Birds cannot reap. Birds cannot gather anything into barns, but you and I can. We are to sow, reap, and gather with the same abandon that a little bird has. The little bird is trusting God to take care of him, and we are to trust Him, also. "Are ye not much better than they?" This does not mean that we shouldn't exercise judgment, because God has given us this ability. Once a Christian asked me, "Do you think a Christian ought to have insurance?" My reply was, "Yes!" Insurance is one means we have today to put our minds at ease concerning the care of our families and ourselves. The important thing is that we are not to go through life with material things becoming a burden to us.

And why take ye thought for raiment? Consider the lilies
of the field, how they grow; they toil not, neither do they
spin [Matt. 6:28].

In this verse the question is asked, "Why take ye thought for raiment?" Think of the time that is consumed by both men and women when it comes to buying clothes. And almost everyone has had the experience at some time of saying, "I can't go tonight, I don't have the right suit or dress to wear." Well, consider the lilies of the field. They cannot toil or spin, and yet God takes care of them. Of course, a Christian should dress as well as he can. To be slovenly in dress or in any action is not honoring to God. Our Lord called attention to the *beauty* of the flowers—

And yet I say unto you, That even Solomon in all his
glory was not arrayed like one of these [Matt. 6:29].

I think He wants us to be as beautiful as possible. Some of us don't have much to work with, but we ought to do the best we can with what we've got.

> **Wherefore, if God so clothe the grass of the field, which to-day is, and to-morrow is cast into the oven, shall he not much more clothe you, O ye of little faith? [Matt. 6:30].**

We are not to be overly anxious about the things of this world. Material things should not be the goal of our life.

> **But seek ye first the kingdom of God, and his righteousness; and all these things shall be added unto you.**
>
> **Take therefore no thought for the morrow: for the morrow shall take thought for the things of itself. Sufficient unto the day is the evil thereof [Matt. 6:33–34].**

"Take . . . no thought for the morrow" means no *anxious* thought. He takes care of the flowers and the birds, and He will take care of you. But the important thing is to put Him first in our life.

As someone has said, "Today is the tomorrow that we worried about yesterday." How true that is for many of us!

CHAPTER 7

THEME: *The relationship of the child of the King with other children of the King maintained by prayer; and final warnings about the two ways, false prophets, false profession, and the two foundations*

JUDGMENT OF OTHERS FORBIDDEN

Judge not, that ye be not judged.

For with what judgment ye judge, ye shall be judged: and with what measure ye mete, it shall be measured to you again [Matt. 7:1–2].

These verses have really been misunderstood. To *judge* can mean "to decide, to distinguish, to condemn, to avenge," and it actually can mean "to damn." These verses do not mean that a child of God is forbidden to judge others, but it does mean that we are not to judge the inward motives of others in the sense of condemning them. We do not know or understand why a brother in Christ does a certain thing. We see only outward acts. God doesn't forbid our judging wrong and evil actions, as we will see. The point is that if you are harsh in your judgments of others, you will be known as the type of person who is severe in his considerations of others. I know this type of person, and I am sure you do, also. Perhaps somebody has said to you, "Don't pay any attention to what he says; he never has a good word to say." You see, he is being judged by the way he judges. This is what our Lord is saying in these verses.

> **And why beholdest thou the mote that is in thy brother's eye, but considerest not the beam that is in thine own eye? [Matt. 7:3].**

He is comparing a little piece of sawdust in your brother's eye to the great big redwood log in your own eye. The "log" is the spirit of criti-

cism and prejudice. With that blocking your vision, you are in no
position to judge the little sin of another.

> **Or how wilt thou say to thy brother, Let me pull out the
> mote out of thine eye; and, behold, a beam is in thine
> own eye?**
>
> **Thou hypocrite, first cast out the beam out of thine own
> eye; and then shalt thou see clearly to cast out the mote
> out of thy brother's eye [Matt. 7:4–5].**

This matter of harsh judgment is certainly something about which we
need to be very careful. Although Jesus makes it clear that we are not
to sit in harsh judgment upon another, He also said that by their fruits
we would know them. The late Dr. James McGinley put it in his rather
unique fashion, "I am no judge, but I am a fruit inspector." And we
can really tell whether or not a Christian is producing fruit.

JUDGMENT OF OTHERS ENJOINED

Now He really puts us on the horns of a dilemma.

> **Give not that which is holy unto the dogs, neither cast ye
> your pearls before swine, lest they trample them under
> their feet, and turn again and rend you [Matt. 7:6].**

We have to determine who the dogs are and who the pigs are, don't
we? These are not four-legged animals He is talking about. We are not
to give that which is holy unto dogs or cast our pearls before swine;
therefore, there is a judgment that we need to make.

There are certain times and places where it is not worthwhile to
say a word. This is a judgment you need to make. I remember a Tennessee legislator friend of mine who was a heavy drinker. He was
wonderfully converted and is a choice servant of God today. The other
members of the legislature knew how he drank. Then they heard he
"got religion," as they called it. One day this fellow took his seat in the
legislature, and his fellow-members looked him over. Finally, some-

one rose, addressed the chairman of the meeting, and said, "I make a motion that we hear a sermon from Deacon So-and-So." Everyone laughed. But my friend was equal to the occasion. He got to his feet and said, "I'm sorry, I do not have anything to say. My Lord told me not to cast my pearls before swine." He sat down, and they never ridiculed him anymore.

A police inspector in the city of New York told me about certain apartments which were filled with no one but homosexuals. He told me, "They know I'm a Christian, and when they are brought into the station, they say to me 'Preach us a sermon!' But I never cast my pearls before swine." He looked at me and said, "I guess you think I'm a little hard-boiled, but I was a flatfoot in that area, and I know those folk. I worked with them for years."

May I say to you, there are swine and there are dogs in our society. What are we to do? Jesus tells us that we are not to judge, and then He tells us we are to judge. Well, He tells us in the next verse what we are to do.

PRAYER, THE WAY OUT OF THE DILEMMA

Ask, and it shall be given you; seek, and ye shall find; knock, and it shall be opened unto you:

For every one that asketh receiveth; and he that seeketh findeth; and to him that knocketh it shall be opened [Matt. 7:7–8].

How to meet the people of this world is the greatest problem facing a child of God. Every day we rub shoulders with princes and paupers, gentlemen and scoundrels, true and false professors. Some folk need our friendship and help, and we need them, and we ought to pull them to our hearts. Others are rascals and will destroy us, and we need to push them from us. How are we to know? To ask, seek, and knock definitely refers to this problem. These verses can be used for other situations also, but it is this situation that they have primary reference to.

While I was a pastor in downtown Los Angeles for twenty-one years, I met people from all walks of life. It took me thirty minutes to drive from my home to the church, and during that time I would tell the Lord I was going to meet some new people during the day and would ask Him to please tell me how I should act with each one. Some people would need my help, but others might try to put a knife in my back. You would be surprised how many times I have been fooled by people. Isn't it interesting that Peter, in the early church, knew Ananias and Sapphira were lying (Acts 5:1–11)? I can never tell when someone is lying. I do not have the spiritual discernment that they had in the early church. I believe it is a gift that only some people have today, and it is important to make discernment a matter of prayer. When you meet new friends, do you ever ask God to make it clear to you how to treat them? I have found out that it is a good idea to do this.

The next verses go on to say that God wants to help you in these matters.

> **Or what man is there of you, whom if his son ask bread, will he give him a stone?**

> **Or if he ask a fish, will he give him a serpent?**

> **If ye then, being evil, know how to give good gifts unto your children, how much more shall your Father which is in heaven give good things to them that ask him? [Matt. 7:9–11].**

Now the so-called Golden Rule comes right in here—

> **Therefore all things whatsoever ye would that men should do to you, do ye even so to them: for this is the law and the prophets [Matt. 7:12].**

All right, when you meet somebody new, how are you going to treat him? You don't know—you are not to judge—but if he is a dog or a swine, you had better know. You have to beware of phonies today. So what do you do? Make it a matter of prayer. "*Therefore* all things whatsoever ye would that men should do to you, do ye even so to them." This is the principle on which you should operate. "Therefore" is the most important word in the Golden Rule. It relates the Golden Rule to that which precedes it. That is, it postulates it on prayer. It all comes together in one package. Don't lift out the Golden Rule and say that you live by it. Understand what the Lord is talking about. Only as we "ask, seek, and knock" are we able to live in the light of the Golden Rule.

THE TWO WAYS

Enter ye in at the strait gate: for wide is the gate, and broad is the way, that leadeth to destruction, and many there be which go in thereat:

Because strait is the gate, and narrow is the way, which leadeth unto life, and few there be that find it [Matt. 7:13-14].

The picture which is given here is not that of a choice between a broad white way with lots of fun and a narrow, dark, uninviting alley. Actually, He is giving a picture of a funnel. If you enter the funnel at the broad end, it keeps narrowing down until you come to death, destruction, and hell. But you can enter the funnel at the narrow part. That's where Christ is—He is the way, the truth, and the life. He says, ". . . I am come that they might have life, and that they might have it more abundantly" (John 10:10). And the longer you walk with Him, the wider it gets. Remember that in Ezekiel's prophecy (ch. 47) there was a river flowing out from the throne of God which began as a little stream and widened out until it became a great river. That pictures the life of a child of God—it gets better every day. This is what our Lord was talking about.

Beware of false prophets, which come to you in sheep's clothing, but inwardly they are ravening wolves.

Ye shall know them by their fruits. Do men gather grapes of thorns, or figs of thistles? [Matt. 7:15–16].

Israel was warned against false prophets, and the church is warned against false teachers, but both classes come in sheep's clothing. "But there were false prophets also among the people, even as there shall be false teachers among you, who privily shall bring in damnable heresies, even denying the Lord that bought them, and bring upon themselves swift destruction" (2 Pet. 2:1). We are to recognize them by their fruits. That is what we are to watch for in their lives.

Not every one that saith unto me, Lord, Lord, shall enter into the kingdom of heaven; but he that doeth the will of my Father which is in heaven [Matt. 7:21].

You can run around and mouth about living by the Golden Rule, but the point is: Are you doing the will of the Father in heaven? If you are doing His will, you'll come to Christ, recognizing that you need a Savior.

Many will say to me in that day, Lord, Lord, have we not prophesied in thy name? and in thy name have we cast out devils? and in thy name done many wonderful works?

And then will I profess unto them, I never knew you: depart from me, ye that work iniquity [Matt. 7:22–23].

Obviously these verses do not refer to believers today. Every believer, living or dead, will be caught up to meet the Lord in the air. None will hear the Lord say, "depart from me." This passage has particular reference to the Great Tribulation period and the Millennium. This is the place to suggest that the Sermon on the Mount will have a particular meaning for the remnant during the Great Tribulation.

Also, there is a needed warning here for professing church members—in fact, for all believers. Folk talk enthusiastically about certain so-called miracle workers today, and they say to me, "You can tell God is with them." In light of these verses, can we be sure of that? The name of Christ is on the lips of many people who are leaders of cults and "isms." Just to use the name of Christ and the Bible is not proof that a system is genuine. It is not the outward profession but the inward relationship to a crucified but living Savior that is all-important.

THE TWO FOUNDATIONS

Therefore whosoever heareth these sayings of mine, and doeth them, I will liken him unto a wise man, which built his house upon a rock:

And the rain descended, and the floods came, and the winds blew, and beat upon that house; and it fell not: for it was founded upon a rock [Matt. 7:24–25].

If you have come to Christ, He is the foundation—"For other foundation can no man lay than that is laid, which is Jesus Christ" (1 Cor. 3:11). When you are resting on Christ, you can build on that foundation. By yielding to the Holy Spirit, you can build a life which the Bible likens to gold, silver, and precious stones.

But there is another kind of building—

And every one that heareth these sayings of mine, and doeth them not, shall be likened unto a foolish man, which built his house upon the sand:

And the rain descended, and the floods came, and the winds blew, and beat upon that house; and it fell: and great was the fall of it [Matt. 7:26–27].

What is that sand? It is human goodness and human effort. It is the old weakness of the flesh. My friend, I say to you that you need something better than the flesh has to offer.

Matthew concludes this section by saying—

**And it came to pass, when Jesus had ended these say-
ings, the people were astonished at his doctrine:**

**For he taught them as one having authority, and not as
the scribes [Matt. 7:28–29].**

Our Lord Jesus was that kind of teacher—He taught with authority; He
wasn't just repeating something He had read. And you and I need to
recognize that we have nothing worthwhile to say unless it is with the
authority of the Word of God and unless we believe it is the Word of
God. I don't want to hear a man who gives me a string of theories,
theories which he himself has never tried and actually knows nothing
about. Today we have a gospel to give, a message of salvation. We
know it works because it has worked in our case. And we have seen it
work in the lives of others who have come to Christ.

My friend, the Sermon on the Mount is a glorious passage of Scripture. Don't bypass it. If you read it aright, it will bring you to the
person of Jesus Christ. It will show you how you fail to measure up to
its precepts. It will show you that you are weak and guilty. It will
make you cry for mercy and will bring you to the person of Christ for
salvation. When you accept Christ as Savior, He will give you the Holy
Spirit who will enable you to live on this high standard.

THE SERMON ON THE MOUNT IN PERSPECTIVE

Now that we have concluded the Sermon on the Mount, I feel that we
need to back off and get a perspective of it because many of my com-
ments may have been new and strange to some folk. A great many
people feel that the Sermon on the Mount states the way believers are
to live in our contemporary society, that it is given to the church.

However, if we step back and look at the Word of God as a whole,
we will see that God has given three great systems by which He is to
govern and rule mankind.

The first one is the Mosaic system, the Law. As you know, early in
Genesis (ch. 7) is the record that God had to destroy the entire human
race (with the exception of one man and his family) because of their

violence and because ". . . every imagination of the thoughts of his heart was only evil continually" (Gen. 6:5). The human family had departed from God, and He had to judge it. Out of the earth He could save only one man and his family, and from these God began a movement toward drawing out of this new population a man who would become the father of a people who would be a witness for Him. Actually, He was going to give them a land, and He was going to make them a great nation—numberless—and He was going to make them a blessing to the world. God, through them, was to reach the world. He gave them through Moses the Mosaic system, and it was a great sacrificial system. The Book of Exodus gives us the details of it and reveals that the very heart of it was the burnt altar where sacrifices were offered. That altar speaks of the Cross of the Lord Jesus Christ, and God never forgave a sin apart from a sacrifice that was made, because, you see, the Law did not save man. It only revealed to man that he was a sinner. It became a system of *condemnation*, not a system of *salvation*. Therefore, throughout the Old Testament the burnt offerings pointed to the coming of the Savior, the Lord Jesus Christ.

Jesus came and offered Himself as the King in order to fulfill the prophecies of the Old Testament. But His nation rejected Him.

The Gospel of Matthew presents Him as King. It is my personal conviction that everything in this Gospel is to be understood in the light of the fact that He is the King. In the Gospel of Matthew, as we have indicated, He was born a King, He lived a King, He died a King, He rose again from the dead as a King, and He is coming again to this earth as a King.

One of the things that He did while He was here on earth was to enunciate a law that was different from the Mosaic Law. It was the so-called Sermon on the Mount, recorded in Matthew 5—7. Excerpts of it are found in the other Gospels, but in Matthew it is given in its fullest extent. As I have mentioned, I am confident that it is an abridged edition, and the evidence of this is that He took two of the Mosaic commandments and lifted them to a higher degree of interpretation than they ever had been held in the Old Testament. For example, He said that if you are angry with your brother, you are guilty of murder. There is nothing about that in the Old Testament. Also, He said that if you so much as look upon a woman to commit adultery in your heart, that you are guilty of it. Believe me, friend, that involves half the human race today. There are very few men who are not guilty of breaking that commandment. Sometime ago a very fine looking woman, a wonderful Christian, and an excellent Bible teacher, told about meeting a certain man, and he happened to be a preacher. She said, "When he looked at me, I could tell what he was doing. He was undressing me, and I think he would have tried to rape me." The man never moved an eyelash, he was just sitting watching the woman approach him. According to the Sermon on the Mount, he was guilty of adultery.

The Sermon on the Mount lifts the Law to the nth degree. Somebody asks, "Isn't that what we are to live by today?" No, it is for the Kingdom which is coming on the earth. At that time we will probably have the unabridged edition of the Sermon on the Mount. It will be the law of the Kingdom, which Christ will set up in the future. There are great principles in it for us, but we have been given a different system. You and I are living in what is called the age of grace or the age of the Holy Spirit. It is a time when God saves by grace, not by keeping a law, not by following a law. We are not saved by anything that we do. Frankly, friend, you are not a Christian until you *believe* something, and that something is ". . . that Christ died for our sins according to the scriptures; And that he was buried, and that he rose again the third day according to the scriptures" (1 Cor. 15:3–4). That is the gospel; that is what saves you.

After you have been saved, God has a way for you to live, and that way is not the Mosaic Law, not the Ten Commandments. Oh, I know what all the great denominations teach. I was brought up and educated in one of them. My Shorter Catechism, when it comes to the subject of sanctification and how to live for God, drags in the Ten Commandments. Suppose you did keep all ten of the commandments (which you don't), that wouldn't save you, because that which saves you is faith in the Lord Jesus Christ. Therefore, the Law cannot save you.

Neither is the Law a way of life; it is not the Christian way of life. Immediately someone asks, "Does that mean you can break it?" Of course it does not give you freedom to break it. It merely means that we have a way of life which is much higher than the Ten Commandments. "But," you may argue, "you have just said that the Sermon on the Mount lifts the Law to the nth degree, so that must be our way of life." No, that's not it. Have you ever stopped to consider if you could keep the Sermon on the Mount?

Are you ready for some startling statements? The Sermon on the Mount has made more hypocrites in the church than anything else. I told you the story of a man who was a church member and an officer but who could cuss like a proverbial sailor, and he thought he was a Christian. When I turned on the light of the Sermon on the Mount, I found that all he did was vote for it; he just approved of it. He didn't keep it. He could not live by it. No one can live by it. You see, it provides a veneer of religion which a great many people assume when their heart is not changed. The *heart* of man has to be changed.

As a result, liberalism is not only found in politics, but liberalism in theology has played a great part. They talk about the fatherhood of God and the brotherhood of man. Well, the Lord Jesus contradicted that theory when He said even to the religious rulers of His day, "Ye are of your father the devil . . ." (John 8:44). Evidently, there were some folk in that day who couldn't call God their Father. The universal fatherhood of God did not apply then, and it does not apply today. Since World War II, the United States has attempted to deal with the world in a spirit of brotherly love. We are hated by many of the nations of the world today and are envied by the rest of them. We have spent literally billions of dollars to buy peace, and we do not have peace in the world today. Why? Because, friend, you cannot run the world by the Sermon on the Mount. We have had politicians who have tried to put these principles to work. Well, aren't the principles good? Of course they are good, but there is something wrong. What is wrong? It is the *heart* of man that is wrong. Man is the problem.

A listener to our radio program wrote, saying, "Dr. McGee, I don't *have* problems; I *am* the problem!" That is the difficulty in the world. There is nothing wrong with the Ten Commandments. They have come from God. They reveal His mind, His will. The Sermon on the

Mount reveals the mind and will of God as well. Certainly, there is nothing wrong with either of those. But there is something radically wrong with mankind.

Listen to the words of the Lord Jesus in the Gospel of Matthew; He will tell you where the problem is. He says, "But those things which proceed out of the mouth come forth from the heart; and they defile the man. For out of the heart proceed evil thoughts, murders, adulteries, fornications, thefts, false witness, blasphemies: these are the things which defile a man: but to eat with unwashen hands defileth not a man" (Matt. 15:18–20).

You can have a religion that requires the washing of hands and body, and you can go through any kind of ritual or liturgy, but the *heart* is the problem. Man has a desperate case of heart trouble today, and jogging won't help him. He needs Jesus, not jogging. The Lord Jesus Christ alone can change the heart by a miracle known as regeneration. He told even a nice, respectable Pharisee by the name of Nicodemus that he must be born again. Although the phrase *born again* is being misused and abused in our day, it is a marvelous, miraculous truth.

My friend, I say to you that you and I have to be regenerated because we've got this old nature. When the Lord Jesus talked about what comes out of the heart, He was not talking about the heart of Joe Doaks, although his is included; He was talking about my heart and your heart. You see, the heart is the problem.

The apostle Paul enlarged upon this fact. He said, "Now the works of the flesh are manifest, which are these; Adultery, fornication, uncleanness, lasciviousness, idolatry, witchcraft, hatred, variance, emulations, wrath, strife, seditions, heresies, envyings, murders, drunkenness, revellings, and such like . . ." (Gal. 5:19–21).

Now we live in a day of situation ethics. We live in a day of gross immorality. People have thrown overboard the so-called Judeo-Christian ethic, and they do as they please. I heard a college professor being interviewed on television. He was asked the question: What is right in our day? His answer was: Anything is right if it makes you feel good. According to that, if it makes you feel good to kill your father and mother, it is perfectly all right.

God gave the Ten Commandments to control the old nature. But they didn't control the old nature because the nation to whom God gave them departed from Him. They went far from God.

Nevertheless, man was not able to measure up to it—Paul repeatedly states this in his epistles.

Now how is man to live? He is not to live by his own effort because he can't make it. The Word says, "But the fruit of the Spirit is love, joy, peace, longsuffering, gentleness, goodness, faith, meekness, temperance [self-control]: against such there is no law" (Gal. 5:22–23). There is no law which can produce these things. It is not naturally in you or me to love—I am not referring to sexual love but to a real concern for others and a real love for God. That kind of love does not come naturally. There used to be a popular song entitled "Doing What Comes Naturally." Well, when man does what comes naturally, he produces our contemporary civilization which is as lawless and as violent as it can be. There is a question in the minds of many serious men in high places concerning whether or not our nation can survive. We cannot, my friend, apart from a restoration of control upon the old nature of man.

How can you produce these wonderful fruits of love, gentleness, meekness, etc.? Well, you cannot produce them by your own effort. Go back to the Sermon on the Mount where it says, "Blessed are the meek: for they shall inherit the earth" (Matt. 5:5). Talk to the Communists about that. Are they inheriting the world by being meek? Ask the people of Afghanistan if the Russian invaders came with meekness. And I received a letter from a missionary in Ethiopia which reveals that the meek are not inheriting the earth. Well, the meek are going to inherit the earth—but not until the King comes, the One who was the meekest Man who ever walked this earth. He is going to come in great power and glory, and He is going to put down unrighteousness upon this earth and establish His Kingdom. When He does that, the Sermon on the Mount will be the law of the Kingdom. But today, how are we to live? By the power of the Spirit; He is the One who produces these wonderful fruits in our lives: love, joy, peace. How about peace in your own heart? Do you have peace with God? Only the Spirit of God can give that to you. And joy—my friend, do you know what it is to have that real joy of the Lord? Then how about this business of meekness? You and I cannot be meek. We have a proud heart. I've got one—I enjoy having folk pat me on the back. Now don't tell me that you don't like it, because you like it too. We are proud. That is the old nature manifesting itself. But the fruit of the Spirit is meekness. All through my ministry I have asked God to make me a meek man—"Oh, God, make me a meek man. Give me humility. Make me the kind of Christian that I ought to be!" I can't do it for myself. God wants to do it for us by the Holy Spirit.

My friend, this is a new way of living. This is not the Mosaic system, this is not the Sermon on the Mount, this is *new!* God has blessed us with all spiritual blessings in the heavenlies—it is spiritual blessings that He has given to us. And now we are to walk through this world in meekness, lowliness of mind and heart, by the power of the Spirit of God.

And today we are to be filled with the Holy Spirit which will enable us to live for God. It will produce fruit in our lives. It will enable us to *serve* God. This is the high plane to which we are called.

It is my hope that you now see the Sermon on the Mount in its true perspective.

Now we are ready to come down from the mount where He enunciated the ethic, and we will see that He also has the dynamic to enforce this law when He comes to rule upon this earth.

CHAPTER 8

THEME: *Jesus demonstrates that He has the dynamic to enforce the ethic of the Sermon on the Mount*

INTRODUCTION

The previous chapter concluded the Sermon on the Mount. It has been conceded by friend and foe alike that there has been given no higher ethic than that in the Sermon on the Mount.

Now the question arises: How can one attain to that high ethic? To answer this question, Matthew brings together a series of miracles which demonstrate that the One who gave the ethic also has the dynamic for its accomplishment. Our Lord made it very clear to us who are believers that ". . . . without me ye can do nothing" (John 15:5). I wish that we could keep that fact before us at all times. You and I, in and of ourselves, are unable to produce anything which is acceptable to God. Christ today works through the Holy Spirit, whom He sent into the world, to accomplish through us what we cannot do.

This reveals an important point: Matthew is not attempting to give us a biography of the Lord Jesus, nor is he attempting to put in chronological order the series of events that took place in His ministry. Rather, he is giving us a movement, which we must not miss. The King went to the mountain, enunciated His manifesto, the law of the Kingdom; now He comes down from the mount, and we see twelve miracles that He performs. This demonstrates that when He rules on this earth, He will have the dynamic to enforce the laws of His Kingdom.

As I have suggested previously, the Sermon on the Mount is probably in an abridged edition. In the Millennium we will have the unabridged, which means that there will be many more things to be carried out.

In chapters 8 and 9 Matthew tells us of twelve miracles. While he does not attempt to give all the miracles that demonstrate the King's power, he gives these in an organized, logical order. Let me call your attention to this in the six miracles recorded in the chapter before us:

1. Healing the leper, our Lord touches him. This is human disease at its worst.
2. Healing the centurion's servant is done from a distance—He has no physical contact with him.
3. Healing Peter's wife's mother, He touches her.
4. Casting out demons, He moves into the supernatural realm of spirits.
5. Stilling the winds and the sea is in the realm of nature and demonstrates His power over natural forces.
6. Casting out demons from the two Gergesenes is a very difficult case in the realm of the spirit world.

The King moves in all of these different areas, and Matthew lists them not in a chronological order but in a logical order. There is a definite movement in Matthew's record.

Now let us turn to the text.

When he was come down from the mountain, great multitudes followed him [Matt. 8:1].

Notice that "great multitudes followed him." There were not just a few folk. You see, He was up in Capernaum, where his headquarters were. And I am confident that the following miracle occurred there. Of course, this raises the question of where He had been when He gave the Sermon on the Mount. I have read many different theories, but I do not think the location is important for us to know. We are told that when He came down from the mountain, great crowds followed Him. Is the King who is able to enunciate the ethic also able to move with power among humanity? That is an important question.

When I was in college, I had a roommate who had gone through a rough year. He was attractive and popular and had fallen in with the wrong crowd. Finally, drinking forced him to quit his ministry. At graduation our speaker carried us into the clouds, telling us what we ought to do, which is what most graduation speakers do. Later, in our room, this fellow dropped down on his bed, dejected, and said, "Mac, I don't need anyone to tell me *what* to do. I need someone to tell me *how* to do it." That, my friend, is what all of us need, isn't it? Now the King has enunciated the ethic; does He have power?

JESUS HEALS A LEPER

And, behold, there came a leper and worshipped him, saying, Lord, if thou wilt, thou canst make me clean [Matt. 8:2].

Notice that Jesus came from the heights to the very depths. Leprosy, symbolic of sin in the Bible, was considered incurable; leprosy was the most loathsome disease. And when this leper came to Jesus, he did not ask, "Will You make me clean?" or "Are You able to make me clean?" This leper had faith. He recognized the lordship of Christ, and on that basis said, "If You will, You can make me clean." What we ask is not always the Lord's will, friend. But if it is His will, He can do it. It is most important that the will of God comes first. It may be easy for you, but it is difficult for me to put the will of God first. I put it like this, "Lord, will You do this because *I* want You to do it?" But the leper says, "I know You can, but will You?" That is, is it according to Your will?

This is a little different from what we hear folk pray today when they *demand* that the Lord do certain things. May I say to you, friend, let *Him* decide—and that's the way it is going to be done anyway.

And Jesus put forth his hand, and touched him, saying, I will; be thou clean. And immediately his leprosy was cleansed [Matt. 8:3].

"Jesus put forth his hand and touched him." If *I* had touched a leper, what would have happened? Well, I might have contracted his disease, and I would not have healed him. But notice what happens. First of all, He did touch him.

Have you ever stopped to think that this man not only had the physical disease of leprosy but that he had a psychological hang-up that was terrible? I do not know this man's background, but I imagine that one day he noticed a breaking out on his hand. Perhaps he had been out plowing, came in, showed his wife, and she put some ointment on it. The next morning it was just as red as it could be, and he went out and plowed again. This went on for about a week, and his wife started getting uneasy. She suggested he visit the priest. He went to the priest who isolated him for fourteen days. At the end of this period of time the disease had spread. The priest told him he had leprosy.

The man asked the priest if he could go and tell his wife and children and say good-bye. The priest said, "I'm sorry, you cannot tell them good-bye. You cannot put your arm around your wife again or hold your children in your arms anymore. When anyone comes near you, you must cry out, 'Unclean, unclean.'" He saw his children grow up from a distance. They would leave food in a certain place, and he would come and get it after they withdrew. He could not touch them. In fact, he had been able to touch no one, and no one had been able to touch him. Then one day he came to Jesus and said, "Lord, if You will, You can make me clean." And what did the Lord Jesus do? He *touched* him. May I say to you that the touch of Jesus was one of the most wonderful things that ever had happened to the man. It not only cleansed his leprosy, but it brought him back into the family of mankind and into the family of God. "Immediately his leprosy was cleansed."

And Jesus saith unto him, See thou tell no man; but go thy way, shew thyself to the priest, and offer the gift that Moses commanded, for a testimony unto them [Matt. 8:4].

In Mark's record we find that this man was so overjoyed—and you can't blame him—that he went out and told everybody he met. He "blazed it abroad!" Consequently, the crowds pushed in on our Lord, and He was forced to retire from the city and stay in desert places.

JESUS HEALS THE CENTURION'S SERVANT

Jesus now enters into the city of Capernaum.

And when Jesus was entered into Capernaum, there came unto him a centurion, beseeching him [Matt. 8:5].

I'm sure the centurion had heard about the leper's healing. The centurion was a Gentile, a captain of sixty centuries (companies of one hundred men) in the Roman legion. Luke's record tells us that he had built a synagogue for the Jews. I have been in the ruins of that old synagogue. (If there is any place in existence where Jesus actually walked, it would be in that old synagogue.) Now hear the centurion's request—

And saying, Lord, my servant lieth at home sick of the palsy, grievously tormented [Matt. 8:6].

This servant was in a very serious condition.

And Jesus saith unto him, I will come and heal him.

The centurion answered and said, Lord, I am not worthy that thou shouldest come under my roof: but speak the word only, and my servant shall be healed.

For I am a man under authority, having soldiers under me: and I say to this man, Go, and he goeth; and to another, Come, and he cometh; and to my servant, Do this, and he doeth it [Matt. 8:7–9].

The centurion was in a position in which he recognized authority. He wore a Roman uniform and could say to a soldier under him, "Do this," and he did it. Why? Because of power, which is authority. He looked at Jesus and said, "You have that kind of power." He recognized that Jesus had that kind of authority over physical illness.

> **When Jesus heard it, he marvelled, and said to them that followed, Verily I say unto you, I have not found so great faith, no, not in Israel [Matt. 8:10].**

It is recorded that on two occasions the Lord Jesus Christ marveled. One was at the unbelief of Israel, and the other was at the faith of this gentile centurion.

> **And I say unto you, That many shall come from the east and west, and shall sit down with Abraham, and Isaac, and Jacob, in the kingdom of heaven [Matt. 8:11].**

It is interesting that He said that many should come from the "east and the west." At the time our Lord said this, my ancestors (and perhaps yours also) were in the west. Or perhaps your ancestors were in the east. Our Lord said that this message was going to get out to them also so that they could trust Him and could "sit down with Abraham, and Isaac, and Jacob, in the kingdom of heaven." What a tremendous statement!

Of course, each individual has to exercise personal faith in Christ. No individual can claim church membership, or family tradition, or the fact that his parents are Christian, for his own salvation.

> **And Jesus said unto the centurion, Go thy way; and as thou hast believed, so be it done unto thee. And his servant was healed in the selfsame hour [Matt. 8:13].**

Although the afflicted servant was not in the presence of Jesus, the centurion's faith in Jesus Christ caused him to be healed. Jesus touched a leper, and he was healed. Now He heals the centurion's servant from a distance.

JESUS HEALS PETER'S WIFE'S MOTHER AND OTHERS

Next we come to the third miracle of healing.

And when Jesus was come into Peter's house, he saw his wife's mother laid, and sick of a fever.

And he touched her hand, and the fever left her: and she arose, and ministered unto them [Matt. 8:14–15].

Peter's mother-in-law was sick with a fever. He touched her and healed her. Notice these three types of diseases. One disease is leprosy, which is incurable. Another affliction is palsy, a paralysis. The other illness is a fever, possibly caused by a temporary illness.

The fourth miracle occurred in the evening.

When the even was come, they brought unto him many that were possessed with devils: and he cast out the spirits with his word, and healed all that were sick [Matt. 8:16].

The word translated "devils" should be *demons*. There are many demons, but there is only one Devil.

Let me call to your attention the fact that they brought "many" to Him. No isolated cases are given. Again I say that if you watch this Gospel record carefully, you will see that Matthew makes it clear that there were literally thousands of people healed in that day. For instance there were thousands of blind men who could now see. There were thousands of crippled folk who were walking around normally. There were thousands of deaf folk who could now hear. This is the reason that the enemies of Jesus never questioned whether or not He had performed miracles. Instead, they asked how He had done them.

That it might be fulfilled which was spoken by Esaias the prophet, saying, Himself took our infirmities, and bare our sicknesses [Matt. 8:17].

This quotation is from Isaiah 53:4. Probably this verse is used by so-called faith healers more than any other verse. They claim that physical healing is in the Atonement, and they use this verse to support their position.

Let's turn the pages back to Isaiah and look at this verse, because I do not believe it gives sanction to the modern healing movement at all. "Surely he hath borne our griefs, and carried our sorrows: yet we did esteem him stricken, smitten of God, and afflicted. But he was wounded for our transgressions, he was bruised for our iniquities: the chastisement of our peace was upon him; and with his stripes we are healed" (Isa. 53:4–5). Of what are we healed? This passage from Isaiah clearly states that we are healed of our transgressions and iniquities. You say to me, "Are you sure about that?" I know this is what these verses are talking about because Peter says: "Who his own self bare our sins in his own body on the tree, that we, being dead to sins, should live unto righteousness: by whose stripes ye were healed" (1 Pet. 2:24). Healed of what? "Sins." Peter is making it very clear that he is talking about *sin*.

"All we like sheep have gone astray; we have turned every one to his own way; and the LORD hath laid on him the iniquity of us all" (Isa. 53:6). It was your *iniquity* and mine which was laid upon Him. Obviously, Isaiah is referring to the fact that Christ would grapple with the great fundamental problem of sin. To contend that healing is in the Atonement is beside the point. So is a glorified body in the Atonement, but I don't have mine yet. Do you? Also, a new earth with the curse removed is in the Atonement of Christ, but it is obvious that we do not have these yet. In this day when sin and Satan still hold sway, there is no release from sickness as an imperative of the Atonement. Why did Paul urge Timothy to take a little wine for his stomach? Why didn't he urge him to get his healing in the Atonement? Why didn't James urge the saints to claim the Atonement when he asked them to call in the elders to pray? (see James 5:13–15). Why didn't Paul claim healing in the Atonement when he mentioned the fact that there was given to him a thorn in the flesh?

"And lest I should be exalted above measure through the abundance of the revelations, there was given to me a thorn in the *flesh*, the messenger of Satan to buffet me, lest I should be exalted above measure. For this thing I besought the Lord thrice, that it might depart from me. And he said unto me, My grace is sufficient for thee: for my strength is made perfect in weakness. Most gladly therefore will I rather glory in my *infirmities,* that the power of Christ may rest upon me" (2 Cor. 12:7–9, italics mine).

There are other examples recorded concerning this subject. Paul, in Philippians, had a regular hospital on his hands. Epaphroditus had been ill (see Phil. 2:25–27), and Paul did not use the Atonement to claim healing.

My friend, we need to face the fact that it is not always God's will to heal. However, sometimes it *is* God's will to heal. Instead of going to a tent or an auditorium where healing services are advertised, why don't you go directly to the Great Physician, the Lord Jesus Christ? Find out if the healing is in His will for you. I believe in divine *healing* but not in so-called divine *healers.* Instead of going to an individual down here on earth who claims to have power, I prefer to take my case to the Great Physician and say with the leper, "If thou wilt, thou canst make me clean" (v. 2). Then whether we are healed or not healed, He gets the glory. And we want Him to have that.

Apparently, Paul knew nothing of this modern cultism of seeking healing in the Atonement. God can and does heal today, but not through so-called faith healers.

Now when Jesus saw great multitudes about him, he gave commandment to depart unto the other side [Matt. 8:18].

Notice the great multitudes of people about Him. Literally, He had healed thousands of afflicted people, and not just those individual cases recorded. John substantiated this fact in his Gospel of John when he wrote: "And many other signs truly did Jesus in the presence of his disciples, which are not written in this book: but these are written, that ye might believe that Jesus is the Christ, the Son of God; and that believing ye might have life through his name" (John 20:30–31).

TWO ASK PERMISSION TO FOLLOW JESUS

Just as Jesus was getting ready to cross to the other side, a man approached Him.

And a certain scribe came, and said unto him, Master, I will follow thee whithersoever thou goest [Matt. 8:19].

This scribe was probably a young man, because an older man most likely would not have acted in this manner. This scribe was in the crowd, toying with the decision to follow Him or not to follow Him. He did not know what to do. Then he saw Jesus preparing to go to the other side. The Lord and His disciples were moving toward the boat, and he had to make up his mind quickly. So he came out from the crowd, apparently fell down before the Lord and said, "I'll follow You wherever You go." The scribe had made his decision. The Lord looked at him and said frankly and candidly:

And Jesus saith unto him, The foxes have holes, and the birds of the air have nests; but the Son of man hath not where to lay his head [Matt. 8:20].

In effect, the Lord Jesus was saying to this young man, "Have you counted the cost?" Our Lord was revealing His poverty when He was here upon this earth. The young man had opened his heart; so our Lord opens His heart. I imagine that He said something like this: It will cost you something to follow Me. When we go to a place, there are no reservations made for us at a Hilton Hotel or a Holiday Inn—we just don't have a place to stay. The birds of the air have nests, and the foxes have holes in the rocks where they can go, but the Son of man has nowhere to lay His head. The poverty of the Lord Jesus! Poverty is part of the curse that He bore.

We are not told that this young man followed Christ. I have always felt that he did. I think that when the boat pulled out, there was a young man in it who had made a decision for Him.

And another of his disciples said unto him, Lord, suffer me first to go and bury my father [Matt. 8:21].

Here is a young man who has made a decision to follow the Lord but wants to bury his father first. This incident has been greatly misunderstood. We get the impression that the old gentleman had just died and that the family was getting ready to hold the funeral service. Our Lord seems very harsh when He replies.

But Jesus said unto him, Follow me; and let the dead bury their dead [Matt. 8:22].

What does the Lord mean by this? How could the dead bury the dead?

Dr. Adam Smith, who was quite an authority on the Middle East, has written several helpful books. He tells of one incident where he wanted to hire an Arab guide. He explained where he wished to go and was told of a young man in a certain village who would be an excellent guide. Dr. Smith went to the village and asked the young man to be his guide and was told, "I first have to bury my father." And there, in front of his hut, sat the old gentleman as hale and hardy as you please. What the young Arab really meant was that he could not leave because he would have to care for his father until he died. The father was the son's responsibility.

The Lord Jesus told the young man who had come to Him to let someone else take care of his father or let the father take care of himself.

Does He impress you as being unfeeling when He said this? I don't think He was. It is my conviction that our Lord was bringing this young man to make a decision. Was he going to put Christ first? When the young man made that decision, the Lord Jesus probably said to him, "Then you go back home and take care of your father."

Many years ago there was a young lady whose father was a demanding old man. She became a missionary, went to a field of service, and did a good work. When she came home after many years, she found her father absolutely helpless. There was no one else to care for him, and he accused her of deserting him and of not being a Christian. Her father had never made a decision for Christ; so she stayed home and made him comfortable and gave him companionship.

The old man was really shaken by it, and during that time he made a decision for Christ. I am confident that the Lord Jesus was leading her in all of that, but there was a day at the beginning when she had to decide whether she would go as a missionary and put Christ first.

That probably was the case of the young man whom Matthew tells us about here.

JESUS STILLS THE TEMPEST ON THE SEA OF GALILEE

And when he was entered into a ship, his disciples followed him [Matt. 8:23].

We have now come to the fifth miracle. It has nothing to do with healing a body but concerns a physical miracle over nature. Here the power of the Lord Jesus is demonstrated, and I believe that Adam had that same power before he lost his dominion. Now we see in the Lord Jesus, the last Adam, the manifestation of this dominion.

And, behold, there arose a great tempest in the sea, insomuch that the ship was covered with the waves: but he was asleep [Matt. 8:24].

This was no ordinary storm. We saw in the account of the temptation of Jesus that the Devil left Him for a little season—but not for long. I think this storm was actually satanic in its origin. This was an attempt of Satan to destroy the Lord.

Notice that our Lord was asleep. This is one of the most human scenes Matthew gives us. Jesus was so weary that even in a storm He could sleep! It reveals something else: He could sleep in a storm whereas I cannot. I'm a little nervous during storms, and so were the disciples—

And his disciples came to him, and awoke him, saying, Lord, save us: we perish [Matt. 8:25].

What little faith they had! Notice how He handled the situation—

And he saith unto them, Why are ye fearful, O ye of little faith? Then he arose, and rebuked the winds and the sea; and there was a great calm [Matt. 8:26].

He rebuked the disciples for their lack of faith, then He rebuked the winds and the sea. The word Luke uses for "rebuke" is *muzzle*. He controlled the waves like we would put a muzzle on a dog. And the waves just smoothed out!

Although it is true that these men exhibited very little faith at this time, there came a day when the storms of persecution broke over the bark of their little lives, and I can't find a record of any one of them crying out, "Carest thou not that we perish?" Rather, we read in Acts 4:29 that they said, "And now, Lord, behold their threatenings: and grant unto thy servants, that with all boldness they may speak thy word." That was the important thing to them. Oh, how we need that kind of courage and conviction in this day in which we live!

Note the profound impression made on His disciples by the miracle of stilling the storm.

But the men marvelled, saying, What manner of man is this, that even the winds and the sea obey him! [Matt. 8:27].

The One who could give the ethic is the One who can also demonstrate the dynamic.

JESUS CASTS THE DEMONS OUT OF TWO GERGESENES

The sixth miracle is a tremendous one. We will not go into detail, but it has to do with the casting out of demons.

And when he was come to the other side into the country of the Gergesenes, there met him two possessed with devils, coming out of the tombs, exceeding fierce, so that no man might pass by that way [Matt. 8:28].

Here Jesus is in Gadara, as it is called today. The people living here were from the tribe of Gad. In the Old Testament, when the land was being divided up among the tribes of Israel, the tribe of Gad stayed on the wrong side of the Jordan River. What happened to them? They went into the pig business, which, as Jews, they should not have done. Once you disobey the Lord, the next step of disobedience is not so difficult. Before long you are walking out of His way and His will altogether.

When Jesus entered into this country, He was met by two men possessed with devils. "Devils" is an unfortunate translation. The word properly and literally is *demons*. These were dangerous men, demon-possessed men.

> **And, behold, they cried out, saying, What have we to do with thee, Jesus, thou Son of God? art thou come hither to torment us before the time? [Matt. 8:29].**

This miracle opens up a tremendous area that, unfortunately, we know so little about today. It is difficult for us to understand the import of this miracle because of our lack of understanding of demons. Personally, I believe the miracles involving demons are the greatest He performed.

> **And there was a good way off from them an herd of many swine feeding.**
>
> **So the devils besought him, saying, If thou cast us out, suffer us to go away into the herd of swine [Matt. 8:30–31].**

For some reason demons want to be brought into physical reality. They seem to be concerned about being materialized. They were even satisfied to indwell a herd of swine.

> **And he said unto them, Go. And when they were come out, they went into the herd of swine: and, behold, the**

whole herd of swine ran violently down a steep place into the sea, and perished in the waters [Matt. 8:32].

The herd of swine, however, would rather die than to have the demons possess them. Mankind is a little different. Many people are demon-possessed today. We had a real manifestation of the supernatural during the time of Moses, during the time of Elijah, and during the time of the Lord Jesus. Today we seem to be moving into an orbit where we are seeing more and more manifestations of that which is demonic. There are many evidences of it all about us. Many instances are difficult to pinpoint, and there is always a danger of going overboard and saying, "I believe So-and-So is demon-possessed." We need to be wary of doing this because it is sort of like witch-hunting. Nevertheless, there are many demon-possessed people today.

When I was in college, I attempted one time to major in abnormal psychology. I knew a man who worked with abnormal people. He was a medical doctor and a Christian, and he told me that he was fairly sure that many of his cases were actually in the realm of the supernatural, cases of demon-possession.

It is interesting to note that the demons did not want to be confined. They knew something of the confinement of certain other demons, the fallen angels, as they are called in the Epistle of Jude. These demons wanted to materialize themselves in this world.

And they that kept them fled, and went their ways into the city, and told every thing, and what was befallen to the possessed of the devils.

And, behold, the whole city came out to meet Jesus: and when they saw him, they besought him that he would depart out of their coasts [Matt. 8:33–34].

This is certainly ironical, is it not? These people would rather have their pigs than Jesus. Believe me, this is not peculiar to the Gadarenes. There are a great many people today who prefer their "pigs" to the Lord Jesus Christ.

CHAPTER 9

THEME: Jesus performs six more miracles; calls Matthew; contends with the Pharisees; continues His ministry in Galilee

In the previous chapter we have seen six miracles which demonstrate that the King has the dynamic, the power, to enforce the ethic He has pronounced, and the chapter before us continues the same thought. We see Him performing physical miracles of healing, one that I classify as supernatural (the raising of the dead) and the spiritual miracle of casting out a demon.

JESUS RETURNS TO CAPERNAUM

And he entered into a ship, and passed over, and came into his own city [Matt. 9:1].

Jesus left the country of the Gadarenes, who did not want Him, and returned to Capernaum.

And, behold, they brought to him a man sick of the palsy, lying on a bed: and Jesus seeing their faith said unto the sick of the palsy: Son, be of good cheer; thy sins be forgiven thee [Matt. 9:2].

We are given details in Mark's account concerning this event. Mark tells us how this man was let down through the roof of a house, and the Lord both healed him and forgave him his sins. Healing and the forgiveness of sins are related.

And, behold, certain of the scribes said within themselves, This man blasphemeth [Matt. 9:3].

The scribes were of the opinion that the Lord could not enable this sick man to walk. The Lord, knowing the thought of their minds and the evil in their hearts, asked them—

> **For whether is easier, to say, Thy sins be forgiven thee; or to say, Arise, and walk? [Matt. 9:5].**

They wouldn't answer His question, but if they had answered, they would have had to say, "Well, for us, one is as great as the other."

> **But that ye may know that the Son of man hath power on earth to forgive sins, (then saith he to the sick of the palsy,) Arise, take up thy bed, and go unto thine house.**
>
> **And he arose, and departed to his house [Matt. 9:6–7].**

When this palsied man got up and walked, it meant that the One who could make him walk was the One who could forgive his sins.

My friend, you and I cannot forgive sins—only the Lord Jesus can do that. And since we cannot forgive sins, we cannot make a man walk. Satan is a deceiver, and we need to investigate the so-called healings we hear about today. Let's don't get in the way of what God does, and let's make sure that He receives the glory.

JESUS CALLS MATTHEW

> **And as Jesus passed forth from thence, he saw a man, named Matthew, sitting at the receipt of custom: and he saith unto him, Follow me. And he arose, and followed him [Matt. 9:9].**

Matthew modestly passes over his call with only this verse. Luke tells us that Matthew made a great dinner in honor of Jesus (see Luke 5:27–29). Evidently the incident which follows took place at this dinner. Matthew invited many of his publican friends to this dinner because he wanted them to know the Lord Jesus Christ also.

And it came to pass, as Jesus sat at meat in the house, behold, many publicans and sinners came and sat down with him and his disciples.

And when the Pharisees saw it, they said unto his disciples, Why eateth your Master with publicans and sinners? [Matt. 9:10–11].

The Pharisees did not believe in eating with publicans and sinners. Many saints today still have the same idea. It doesn't hurt to invite sinners to dinner because they are the ones who need to be reached for Christ. We need to have some contact with sinners.

But when Jesus heard that, he said unto them, They that be whole need not a physician, but they that are sick [Matt. 9:12].

Jesus is the Great Physician. He has come to heal mankind of their basic problem, which is sin. This ought to be said to a lot of our little Christian groups who have their banquets and "fellowship" meetings and do not invite the unsaved. If the unsaved do come, the majority of the Christians freeze them out anyway. May I say to you that I think some of these so-called Christian groups are *sinful* in their very existence and in the way they meet today.

But go ye and learn what that meaneth, I will have mercy, and not sacrifice: for I am not come to call the righteous, but sinners to repentance [Matt. 9:13].

Matthew is at it again, quoting Hosea 6:6 from the Old Testament.

When Jesus said, "For I am not come to call the righteous, but sinners to repentance," He could have included the Pharisees because they were sinners. In fact, all of us are included—"For *all* have sinned, and come short of the glory of God" (Rom. 3:23, italics mine).

PARABLE OF OLD GARMENT AND OLD BOTTLES

Then came to him the disciples of John, saying, Why do we and the Pharisees fast oft, but thy disciples fast not? [Matt. 9:14].

The disciples of John had been observing the Lord Jesus. After all, some of these men were originally disciples of John—we know that Andrew and Philip were. They had come and were following the Lord Jesus, and the other disciples of John said, "Look, here is something happening which is a little different from the way we do it, and we wonder why."

John, as has been indicated previously, was an Old Testament prophet. He walked out of the Old Testament into the New Testament to make the announcement that the Messiah had come. Malachi had predicted that a messenger would come to prepare the way for the Lord Jesus Christ. John said, "All I'm doing is getting the highway ready for the Lord. He will be here in a few minutes." And He did come as John had said.

Now our Lord is going to enunciate a great principle and reveal the fact that the dispensation is going to be changed.

And Jesus said unto them, Can the children of the bride-chamber mourn, as long as the bridegroom is with them? but the days will come, when the bridegroom shall be taken from them, and then shall they fast [Matt. 9:15].

Although for believers today fasting has real value, we have been given no commandment to fast. Fasting should be done with the idea that we are prostrating ourselves before God because we are in need of His mercy and of His help. This is the thought behind fasting.

Now listen to the Lord as He explains the change of dispensations from the Old Testament of law to the New Testament of grace.

> No man putteth a piece of new cloth unto an old gar-
> ment, for that which is put in to fill it up taketh from the
> garment, and the rent is made worse.
>
> Neither do men put new wine into old bottles: else the
> bottles break, and the wine runneth out, and the bottles
> perish: but they put new wine into new bottles, and both
> are preserved [Matt. 9:16–17].

Our Lord is saying this: The old covenant, the old dispensation of law, was ending, and He had not come to project it or to continue under that dispensation. Actually, He had come to provide a new garment, and that new garment was the robe of righteousness which He gives to those who do nothing more than to trust Him.

The "bottles" were the wineskins of that day. They were fashioned of animal skin. You can see that when new wine would be put into a new wineskin, it would expand. But an old wineskin had reached the place of maximum expansion; when it was filled with new wine, it would naturally burst open and the wine would be lost.

Our Lord is saying this, "I haven't come to sew patches on an old garment. I have come to present a new garment, something which is altogether new." This was very radical. John summed it up in his Gospel when he said, "For the law was given by Moses, but grace and truth came by Jesus Christ" (John 1:17).

JESUS HEALS A WOMAN AND RAISES
A CHILD FROM THE DEAD

We come to the eighth and ninth miracles which, in a manner of speaking, are linked together. Both are miracles of healing, and it is a tremendous scene.

> While he spake these things unto them, behold, there
> came a certain ruler, and worshipped him, saying, My
> daughter is even now dead: but come and lay thy hand
> upon her, and she shall live [Matt. 9:18].

Luke in his Gospel tells us that when this ruler first came to Jesus it was to ask Him to heal his daughter: "And, behold, there came a man named Jairus, and he was a ruler of the synagogue: and he fell down at Jesus' feet, and besought him that he would come into his house: For he had one only daughter, about twelve years of age, and she lay a dying . . ." (Luke 8:41–42). The little girl was sick unto death, and while her father waited to talk with Jesus, a servant came and told him that the little girl had died.

> **And Jesus arose, and followed him, and so did his disciples [Matt. 9:19].**

As Jesus and His disciples arose to follow Jairus to his home, a large crowd gathered around Him.

> **And, behold, a woman, which was diseased with an issue of blood twelve years, came behind him, and touched the hem of his garment [Matt. 9:20].**

You cannot help but notice how striking this passage is. The little girl was twelve years old, and this woman had suffered with this issue of blood for twelve years. Here were twelve years of light going out of this child's life, and twelve years of darkness were coming to an end and light was breaking into this woman's life. Here is the contrast of light and darkness.

In the previous verse note what the woman did—Jesus did not touch her, as He did in many other miracles, but she touched Him. It was not the method, however, that brought about her healing; it was her faith.

> **For she said within herself, If I may but touch his garment, I shall be whole.**

> **But Jesus turned him about, and when he saw her, he said, Daughter, be of good comfort; thy faith hath made thee whole. And the woman was made whole from that hour [Matt. 9:21–22].**

Dr. Luke gives us much more detail about this miracle, recording our
Lord's reaction to this woman's touch and her response. Jesus then
moves from this woman and continues toward the house of Jairus.

> **And when Jesus came into the ruler's house, and saw
> the minstrels and the people making a noise,**
>
> **He said unto them, Give place: for the maid is not dead,
> but sleepeth. And they laughed him to scorn [Matt.
> 9:23-24].**

When Jesus arrived at the home, people were already mourning for the
child. He told them the little girl was only sleeping and not dead, and
they laughed at Him. None in the house believed Jesus could raise the
dead, but He kept moving toward the child.

> **But when the people were put forth, he went in, and
> took her by the hand, and the maid arose [Matt. 9:25].**

This is the first instance of raising the dead that we have in the Gospels. Three notable incidents of raising the dead are recorded. Again,
Luke goes into more detail than Matthew. Luke adds that He spoke to
the little girl in this lovely fashion, "Little lamb, wake up, I say." The
method of Jesus in raising the dead was always the same. He spoke to
the person directly.

After healing the woman with the issue of blood and raising Jairus'
daughter from the dead, the fame of Jesus spread.

> **And the fame hereof went abroad into all that land
> [Matt. 9:26].**

JESUS OPENS THE EYES OF TWO BLIND MEN

The tenth miracle concerns two blind men who followed the Lord
Jesus—

> And when Jesus departed thence, two blind men fol-
> lowed him, crying, and saying, Thou Son of David, have
> mercy on us [Matt. 9:27].

Note that the two blind men addressed Him as the "Son of David."
This is significant in this Gospel which presents Him as King.

> And when he was come into the house, the blind men
> came to him: and Jesus saith unto them, Believe ye that I
> am able to do this? They said unto him, Yea, Lord.

> Then touched he their eyes, saying, According to your
> faith be it unto you.

> And their eyes were opened; and Jesus straitly charged
> them, saying, See that no man know it [Matt. 9:28-30].

This is another remarkable case where the Lord charges these men not
to tell anyone about what happened to them. He said the same thing to
the leper. There are several reasons for the Lord to ask this favor, but
one is made clear in this passage. The publication of His miracles
caused the crowds to press in upon Him and actually hindered Him at
His work.

> But they, when they were departed, spread abroad his
> fame in all that country [Matt. 9:31].

These two men whose sight was restored just couldn't contain their
joy—"they . . . spread abroad his fame."

JESUS HEALS A MAN DUMB AND
DEMON-POSSESSED

We now come to the eleventh miracle. Another demon-possessed
man is healed. This is the third incident of demon possession recorded in chapters 8—9 of Matthew.

> As they went out, behold, they brought to him a dumb man possessed with a devil.
>
> And when the devil was cast out, the dumb spake: and the multitudes marvelled, saying, It was never so seen in Israel [Matt. 9:32–33].

Notice the reaction of the Pharisees—

> But the Pharisees said, He casteth out devils through the prince of the devils [Matt. 9:34].

They did not deny that He had caused the dumb to speak and the blind to see and the crippled to walk. What they accused Him of was that He did these things by the power of Satan.

> And Jesus went about all the cities and villages, teaching in their synagogues, and preaching the gospel of the kingdom, and healing every sickness and every disease among the people [Matt. 9:35].

"The gospel of the kingdom" is not the gospel of the grace of God. This does not mean to imply that there are two gospels. There is only one gospel, but there are many facets of it. The gospel of the Kingdom was the announcement that the Kingdom of the heavens was at hand. It meant to get ready for the King. It required a heart condition that would accept and follow the King who was then going to the cross.

"And healing every sickness and every disease among the people." We see again and again that Matthew inserts this information that there were thousands of folk who were healed in that day. This is the reason the enemy never questioned the fact that He performed miracles—it was too obvious.

Again let me say that in our day a great many people get excited about the claim of certain ones to have a gift of healing. Personally, I do not think that anyone in our day has that gift. As I mentioned previously, for many years I have offered one hundred dollars to anyone who would come forward and be able to prove that he had been healed by a so-called faith healer. You would think that out of literally hundreds of reported faith healings during the time of a sensational healing meeting, there would be one case that is genuine. I'll be honest with you—I did expect someone to come along that had had a psychological cure. No one has come.

I asked the leader of a certain denomination who has offered one thousand dollars to anyone who could prove he had been cured by a faith healer what his experience had been. He told me about several lawsuits that had been filed against him by those who had tried to collect the money. No one, however, had ever been able to go into court and prove that he had been healed by a faith healer.

In contrast to this, there were thousands of folk who had been healed by our Lord when He was here. And I would think that there would be at least one today, wouldn't you think so? Let me ask you the question: Do you really *know* someone who has been healed by a man or woman? The point is that the Lord Jesus Christ is the Great Physician, and I believe—I *know*—that He can heal today as well as yesterday. I have great confidence in Him. Now let me make myself clear: We should seek the best medical help available to us, but we need to recognize that doctors are very limited. However, the Lord Jesus is not limited. We can be confident that He will deal with us according to His perfect will, and we need to give Him the credit for whatever happens.

But when he saw the multitudes, he was moved with compassion on them, because they fainted, and were scattered abroad, as sheep having no shepherd [Matt. 9:36].

The note of compassion which concludes this chapter is startling, isn't it?

God's ideal kings and rulers have been shepherds. Both Moses and David were shepherds before they led God's people. When we pray for the Lord to thrust forth laborers into His harvest, pray that He will give them *the heart of a shepherd*. Pray that the Lord will give you a heart of compassion for the lost.

> **Then saith he unto his disciples, The harvest truly is plenteous, but the labourers are few;**
>
> **Pray ye therefore the Lord of the harvest, that he will send forth labourers into his harvest [Matt. 9:37–38].**

Having said this to His disciples, He now sends them forth. My friend, when you pray for something, it is always well to be willing to do it yourself. When our Lord asked the disciples to pray for laborers, He sent into the harvest these very men whom He asked to pray about it. This is very interesting indeed. An old bishop in the Methodist church in Georgia years ago said, "When a man prays for a corn crop, the Lord expects him to say 'Amen' with a hoe." I have always believed that you should not pray about anything unless you are also willing to do it yourself.

CHAPTER 10

THEME: Jesus commissions the twelve apostles to go to the nation Israel and preach the gospel of the Kingdom

This chapter continues the movement we have seen in the Gospel of Matthew. The Lord Jesus, having given the ethic, came down from the mountain, demonstrated His power in the twelve miracles which have been enumerated. Now He commissions the twelve apostles to go to the nation Israel and preach the gospel of the Kingdom.

These men are to go, not as forerunners but as after-runners. Our Lord gave them power to perform miracles—this was their credential. (Have you ever noticed that John the Baptist never performed a miracle?) Note that their title is changed from disciple (learner) to apostle (delegate).

As we enter this chapter, keep in mind the number of cults which come to this chapter for their authority for some peculiar ministry or conduct. You see, the instructions for the Christian are not found in this chapter. We need to consider the instruction here in light of the circumstances and conditions under which they were given, and we should be able to interpret them accurately.

THE TWELVE COMMISSIONED AND NAMED

And when he had called unto him his twelve disciples, he gave them power against unclean spirits, to cast them out, and to heal all manner of sickness and all manner of disease [Matt. 10:1].

The power He gave to them was their credential as they went to the nation Israel. The prophets of the Old Testament had said that this would be the credentials of the Messiah. Having given them this power, they are no longer disciples but apostles.

Now the names of the twelve apostles are these; The first, Simon, who is called Peter, and Andrew his brother; James the son of Zebedee, and John his brother;

Philip, and Bartholomew; Thomas, and Matthew the publican; James the son of Alphaeus, and Lebbaeus, whose surname was Thaddaeus;

Simon the Canaanite, and Judas Iscariot, who also betrayed him [Matt. 10:2-4].

THE METHOD AND MESSAGE OF THE TWELVE

These twelve Jesus sent forth, and commanded them, saying, Go not into the city of the Gentiles, and into any city of the Samaritans enter ye not.

But go rather to the lost sheep of the house of Israel [Matt. 10:5-6].

Now if you are going to take your instructions from this chapter for your personal ministry, you will have to limit yourself to the nation Israel, because this is to be given to the "lost sheep of the house of Israel." Obviously, these verses do not contain our commission. Contrast it with our commission in Acts 1:8: ". . . and ye shall be witnesses unto me both in Jerusalem, and in all Judaea, and in Samaria, and unto the uttermost part of the earth." Notice that we are to include Samaria and the uttermost part of the earth, while Jesus instructed the twelve in this chapter to stay out of Samaria and not to go into the way of the Gentiles but only to "the lost sheep of the house of Israel."

And the message of the twelve was to be this:

And as ye go, preach, saying, The kingdom of heaven is at hand [Matt. 10:7].

How could it be "at hand"? It was at hand in the person of the King— He was in their midst.

At the turn of the century and at the conclusion of the Victorian era, there was a feeling of optimism throughout the so-called Christian world. All of the major denominations at that time took on the herculean task of "building the Kingdom of Heaven" here on this earth. Each group thought that they had a contract from God to accomplish this purpose. Of course, the church was never called to build the Kingdom. The Lord Jesus Christ Himself will establish the Kingdom when He returns to the earth. The church is a called-out body from the world to manifest Christ and to preach His gospel throughout the world. Kingdom business is none of our business.

The Kingdom of Heaven is within us when we receive Christ.

Now notice that our Lord sends out the twelve with the same credentials that He Himself has—

Heal the sick, cleanse the lepers, raise the dead, cast out devils: freely ye have received, freely give [Matt. 10:8].

Now I insist that if you are going to do one of the above things, you ought to be able to do all four of them. Note that raising the dead is included! Obviously, this was applicable to the time and circumstances under which it was given.

It is interesting to note that folk in our day who use verse 8 as their commission ignore the next verse—at least, I have never heard them use it—yet it all goes together in one package.

Provide neither gold, nor silver, nor brass in your purses [Matt. 10:9].

Some time ago I suggested to a so-called faith healer that he go to the hospitals where they really needed him. But it is interesting to see that these folk have to be in a place where an offering can be taken.

Obviously, we need to place this verse in its correct context. These were temporary instructions during our Lord's three-year ministry. There came a day at the end of His ministry when He gave different instructions to His apostles: "And he said unto them, When I sent you without purse, and scrip, and shoes, lacked ye any thing? And they said, Nothing. Then said he unto them, But now, he that hath a purse, let him take it, and likewise his scrip: and he that hath no sword, let him sell his garment, and buy one" (Luke 22:35–36).

And the apostle Paul wrote, "Even so hath the Lord ordained that they which preach the gospel should live of the gospel" (1 Cor. 9:14), and he deals at length with the matter of the preacher in 1 Corinthians 9. In our day, certainly God expects us to support Christian ministries.

My only suggestion is that if you are going to appropriate to yourself Matthew 10:8, be sure to take the next verse that goes along with it. I don't mean to be harsh, but it is important to interpret a verse in its context.

Now notice the further instructions our Lord gave to the twelve before He sent them out at this time—

> **And into whatsoever city or town ye shall enter, inquire who in it is worthy; and there abide till ye go thence [Matt. 10:11].**

This certainly is not for our day. The best place for a visiting speaker to go is to a motel or hotel instead of causing an extra burden on folk when they are so busy. Some people still have a "prophet's chamber," and I know where many of them are in this country; they are delightful places. But in our day, I don't think our Lord would have us go into a town and ask, "Who is worthy in this town; who is your outstanding Christian?" then go and knock on his door and say, "Look, I'm here." Again let's note that the Lord Jesus is giving His men temporary instructions under local circumstances for a three-year period. Let's interpret it in its correct context.

> **And when ye come into an house, salute it.**

> **And if the house be worthy, let your peace come upon it: but if it be not worthy, let your peace return to you [Matt. 10:12–13].**

The word *house* refers, of course, not to the building but to the people who live in it, the household.

And whosoever shall not receive you, nor hear your words, when ye depart out of that house or city, shake off the dust of your feet [Matt. 10:14].

This is not our commission today. This is not the attitude of modern missionaries. Certainly, when I have gone to other places to hold meetings, I have never gone outside the towns and shaken the dust off my feet. I won't say that I haven't felt like it in some places, but I have never done it. I feel that this instruction was given to these men for that particular time.

Verily I say unto you, It shall be more tolerable for the land of Sodom and Gomorrha in the day of judgment, than for that city [Matt. 10:15].

In the next chapter of Matthew we will find out what happened to some of these cities that fell under judgment.

WHAT THE TWELVE MUST EXPECT

Behold, I send you forth as sheep in the midst of wolves: be ye therefore wise as servants, and harmless as doves [Matt. 10:16].

Having spoken about the local situation, the Lord now gives these men certain great principles by which they are to go as His witnesses. These *principles* are good for time and eternity, and they certainly are good for our day. The child of God should be wise as a serpent and harmless as a dove. It is dangerous to be one and not the other. I have met some who are wise as serpents—they are clever—but they are not helpless as doves. To use a common expression, they will *take* you. I know others who are quite gullible; they are harmless as doves, but they are not wise as serpents. A serpent is dangerous, and a dove is in danger, so that we need to combine both qualities.

> **But beware of men: for they will deliver you up to the councils, and they will scourge you in their synagogues [Matt. 10:17].**

I have never been scourged in a synagogue, but I have been verbally scourged in some of our good churches.

> **And ye shall be brought before governors and kings for my sake, for a testimony against them and the Gentiles [Matt. 10:18].**

In that day this certainly happened to those who were His. Also, it has happened subsequently to many in the church.

> **But when they deliver you up, take no thought how or what ye shall speak: for it shall be given you in that same hour what ye shall speak.**

> **For it is not ye that speak, but the Spirit of your Father which speaketh in you [Matt. 10:19–20].**

I believe these verses apply to those men who had no opportunity to prepare answers when they were arrested for doing the job Jesus sent them to do. These men sent out by the Lord made no preparation, and if we place these verses in the local situation, we will have no problem with them at all.

Unfortunately, there are many folk who apply these verses to themselves and make no preparation for their sermons! When I was in seminary, a fellow student, who was a little odd in more ways than one, believed that he should preach without any preparation. A friend and I decided one night that we would go and hear him preach. Well, it was painfully obvious that he had not prepared his message. On the way back to the seminary, my friend, who had even more nerve than I had, asked him, "Did you prepare that message tonight?"

"Of course, I didn't!"

"Well, how did you get it?"

"The Spirit of God gave it to me."

My friend said to him, "I don't think you ought to blame that message on the Holy Spirit!"

Another friend of mine was at Temple, Texas, years ago when the trains were running through there, and he had to change trains there on a Sunday morning. As he waited for his connection, he was walking up and down with his notes in his hand because he was to preach that morning. He was wearing a long frock coat, and another man approached him who also was wearing a frock coat. The man asked him, "Are you a preacher?"

"Yes."

"What are you doing there?"

"I'm going over my notes for my sermon this morning."

"Do you mean to tell me that you *prepare* your sermons?"

"Yes, don't you?"

"No. I just get up and let the Holy Spirit speak through me."

"Well, suppose when you get up, the Holy Spirit doesn't give you the message immediately. Then what do you do?"

"Oh," he said. "I just mess around until He does!"

Unfortunately, there are a whole lot of preachers just messing around in our day and using as their excuse this instruction which our Lord gave to His apostles. That is really a misinterpretation of Scripture. If we put these verses back in their context and see them in their local situation, their meaning is crystal clear.

Jesus continues:

And the brother shall deliver up the brother to death, and the father the child: and the children shall rise up against their parents, and cause them to be put to death [Matt. 10:21].

The coming of Christ into the world divided man; it did not bring unity. When one person in a family accepts Christ and another family member does not, you have a division. Paul said it well in

1 Corinthians 1:18, "For the preaching of the cross is to them that perish foolishness; but unto us which are saved it is the power of God."

> **And ye shall be hated of all men for my name's sake: but he that endureth to the end shall be saved [Matt. 10:22].**

This refers to the fact that the Lord will be able to keep His own for the three-year period of His ministry. Similarly, Matthew 24:13 means that the Lord will be able to keep His own during the Great Tribulation period, as we shall see when we come to chapter 24.

> **But when they persecute you in this city, flee ye into another: for verily I say unto you, Ye shall not have gone over the cities of Israel, till the Son of man be come [Matt. 10:23].**

Notice that He says, "Ye shall not have gone over the cities of *Israel*"— not the world, but *Israel*—"till the Son of man be come," meaning until He is manifested before the nation. It is difficult for us to conceive of the fact that our Lord *covered* the nation of Israel. And there was a real division in the nation concerning Him. When He asked His disciples, ". . . Whom do men say that I the Son of man am?" (Matt. 16:13), they gave Him several answers. Everybody had his own opinion about Him. In our day He is still the most controversial Person who has ever been in the world.

PRINCIPLES THAT ARE TO GOVERN
THE LIVES OF ALL DISCIPLES

Now the Lord Jesus gives His men general instructions. Again, these are great principles which you and I can certainly apply to ourselves, although the direct interpretation is to the twelve apostles.

> **The disciple is not above his master, nor the servant above his lord [Matt. 10:24].**

We need to keep in mind that we are representing the Lord Jesus Christ, and He must come first. If we do not put Him first, we will have trouble—I mean trouble with *Him!*

> **It is enough for the disciple that he be as his master, and the servant as his lord. If they have called the master of the house Beelzebub, how much more shall they call them of his household? [Matt. 10:25].**

Don't worry about what people say about you if you are being faithful to Him. They did not say nice things about the Lord. If Jesus Himself received ill-treatment, His disciples could hardly expect to fare better.

> **Fear them not therefore: for there is nothing covered, that shall not be revealed; and hid, that shall not be known [Matt. 10:26].**

Friend, your life is going to be turned wrong side out someday and so is mine. God's ultimate judgment will someday vindicate believers and deal with persecutors; so you had better have the inside of your life looking as attractive as the outside.

> **What I tell you in darkness, that speak ye in light: and what ye hear in the ear, that preach ye upon the house-tops [Matt. 10:27].**

I always think of a radio as being the best way of preaching from the housetops. Put an aerial on your rooftop and you can pick up even the most difficult radio stations. This is the way we preach from the housetops today, and I think it is an effective way.

> **And fear not them which kill the body, but are not able to kill the soul: but rather fear him which is able to destroy both soul and body in hell [Matt. 10:28].**

In other words, fear God.

Someone asked Cromwell why he was such a brave man. Cromwell replied, "I've learned that when you fear God, you do not have any man to fear."

> **Are not two sparrows sold for a farthing? and one of them shall not fall on the ground without your Father [Matt. 10:29].**

What a marvelous verse! The Lord takes care of the little sparrows. Have you ever watched a sparrow? I was in a hotel back East, in a downtown area, and there were hundreds of sparrows around a fountain on the grounds. I thought to myself, "There is not one of those birds that the Lord does not know about." How wonderful this is to remember.

> **But the very hairs of your head are all numbered [Matt. 10:30].**

God loves you! The Lord Jesus loves you more than your mother loved you. Did your mother ever count the hairs on your head? But God knows the number!

> **Fear ye not therefore, ye are of more value than many sparrows [Matt. 10:31].**

Think of that—if God knows where the sparrow is, my friend, He knows where you are. You will never get to the place where He doesn't know where you are.

> **Whosoever therefore shall confess me before men, him will I confess also before my Father which is in heaven.**

> **But whosoever shall deny me before men, him will I also deny before my Father which is in heaven [Matt. 10:32–33].**

It stands to reason that if we have accepted the Lord Jesus Christ as our personal Savior from sin, we will acknowledge it publicly or whenever it is deemed necessary to give a testimony. Therefore, the statement of verse 33 follows as day follows night. This verse alerts me to want to confess Him and never to deny Him. However, I don't want to make a fool of myself because there are times when I am not to cast my pearls before swine; that is, there are times when we do not honor Him by the use of His name in certain circles. Assuredly, we never want to deny Him—neither *will* we deny Him.

Think not that I am come to send peace on earth: I came not to send peace, but a sword [Matt. 10:34].

This is a verse with which the pacifist has had difficulty. However, until all unrighteousness is put down and suppressed, the Person of Christ will cause the enmity of Satan, and a battle will ensue.

I wish a little of this verse would get into the United Nations today and into the thinking of some liberal preachers. Christ did not come to bring peace at His first coming. Sin is still in the world; and, as long as it stays upon the earth, God says that there will be no peace for the wicked.

For I am come to set a man at variance against his father, and the daughter against her mother, and the daughter in law against her mother in law.

And a man's foes shall be they of his own household [Matt. 10:35–36].

Paul amplified the truth of this verse when he said, "For the preaching of the cross is to them that perish foolishness; but unto us which are saved it is the power of God" (1 Cor. 1:18). Actually, families have been divided by the preaching of the gospel. Also, brothers have been separated. There is a unity of believers, and that very unity makes a division with the unsaved world.

> He that loveth father or mother more than me is not worthy of me: and he that loveth son or daughter more than me is not worthy of me [Matt. 10:37].

Unless you have really committed your life to Christ and paid a price, you cannot talk much about commitment. Personally, I do not brag about being a committed Christian because I find that I am in Simon Peter's class. But, thank God, *He* is faithful. That's the wonder of it all!

> And he that taketh not his cross, and followeth after me is not worthy of me [Matt. 10:38].

I wish that I could have heard Him use that expression, "not worthy of me." Many of us are not, and it means that He is not going to use us unless we are really committed to Him. But, thank God, He will not throw us overboard!

> He that findeth his life shall lose it: and he that loseth his life for my sake shall find it [Matt. 10:39].

He is putting in contrast the life which we have here in the flesh with the gift of eternal life which comes through faith in the Lord Jesus Christ. It is possible that when a person comes to Christ, he may be put to death because of his faith. This is not true in the United States yet, but it is true in other parts of the world even in our day. A man who loses his physical life for Christ shall find eternal life which takes him into the presence of Christ. "We are confident, I say, and willing rather to be absent from the body, and to be present with the Lord" (2 Cor. 5:8).

> He that receiveth you receiveth me, and he that receiveth me receiveth him that sent me.
>
> He that receiveth a prophet in the name of a prophet shall receive a prophet's reward; and he that receiveth a righteous man in the name of a righteous man shall receive a righteous man's reward.

And whosoever shall give to drink unto one of these little ones a cup of cold water only in the name of a disciple, verily I say unto you, he shall in no wise lose his reward [Matt. 10:40–42].

In John 15 the Lord Jesus clarifies this section when He says that the world has hated Him and is going to hate His own. We ought not to be any more popular with the world than Jesus Christ is popular. The measure of our loyalty and faithfulness to Him is given in the prophet's reward and the righteous man's reward. If you defend the Lord Jesus as a prophet, you will receive a prophet's reward. If you receive Him as only a righteous man, you will receive a righteous man's reward. But if you acknowledge Him as Lord and Savior, you will receive a full reward. Our Lord makes it very clear that rewards are given on the basis of faithfulness.

CHAPTER 11

THEME: Jesus continues His ministry; is quizzed by
the disciples of John; rejects the cities where He has
performed mighty works, and issues a new invitation
to individuals

The movement continues in this chapter. The Lord Jesus has enunciated the ethic, He has performed the miracles, and He has sent
His disciples out to present His claims—they have gone down the
highways and byways until they have covered all the cities of Israel.
Now what is the reception? What is the reaction to His messianic
claim? Let me give it to you in one word: *rejection!*

This chapter makes a turning point in the ministry of the Lord
Jesus Christ. In verses 28–30 we will see that He gives a new message.
It is a definite departure from the message of repentance in view of the
presence of the King.

> **And it came to pass, when Jesus had made an end of
> commanding his twelve disciples, he departed thence to
> teach and to preach in their cities [Matt. 11:1].**

Having sent out His disciples, He Himself goes out. How important it
was to get the Word of God out to the people! And in our day it is
equally important.

JESUS QUIZZED BY THE DISCIPLES OF JOHN

> **Now when John had heard in the prison the works of
> Christ, he sent two of his disciples [Matt. 11:2].**

Back in Matthew 4:12 it is recorded that John the Baptist was put in
prison. So he has been imprisoned for a while now, but he has been
kept informed about the movements of the Lord Jesus. John's disciples

have been watching Jesus and reporting to John. John is expecting any day for the door of his prison to be opened, because he believes that Jesus is coming immediately to the throne to establish His Kingdom.

And said unto him, Art thou he that should come, or do we look for another? [Matt. 11:3].

John's question is a logical one. He has every reason to believe that the King would have assumed power by this time. He is definitely puzzled that the Lord is moving so slowly toward the throne.

Note the Lord's answer to John.

Jesus answered and said unto them, Go and shew John again those things which ye do hear and see:

The blind receive their sight, and the lame walk, the lepers are cleansed, and the deaf hear, the dead are raised up, and the poor have the gospel preached to them.

And blessed is he, whosoever shall not be offended in me [Matt. 11:4–6].

The answer of Jesus is remarkable and can be understood only in light of the credentials which the Old Testament said the Messiah would have. This is a direct reference to Isaiah 35:4–6:"Say to them that are of a fearful heart, Be strong, fear not: behold, your God will come with vengeance, even God with a recompence; he will come and save you. Then the eyes of the blind shall be opened, and the ears of the deaf shall be unstopped. Then shall the lame man leap as an hart, and the tongue of the dumb sing: for in the wilderness shall waters break out, and streams in the desert."

Now waters did not break out in the wilderness nor were there streams in the desert when Jesus came. Why? Because He did not establish the Kingdom when He came the first time. But He was the King, and He had the credentials of the Messiah—that is all He is saying. John would recognize the credentials.

JESUS PAYS TRIBUTE JOHN THE BAPTIST

In the following verses the Lord Jesus defends John in case anyone wanted to criticize him.

> **And as they departed, Jesus began to say unto the multitudes concerning John, What went ye out into the wilderness to see? A reed shaken with the wind? [Matt. 11:7].**

By the way, John was not the reed shaken with the wind; he was a wind shaking the reeds! In our day, the pulpit has become very weak because it is in subjection to somebody sitting out there in the pew who doesn't like the preacher. Or the message is tailored to suit a certain group in the church. Too often the pulpit is a reed that is shaken in the wind. Thank God for John the Baptist, a wind shaking the reeds!

Our Lord continues His commendation of John the Baptist—

> **But what went ye out for to see? A man clothed in soft raiment? behold, they that wear soft clothing are in kings' houses [Matt. 11:8].**

John the Baptist was rugged, a rugged individual!

> **But what went ye out for to see? A prophet? yea, I say unto you, and more than a prophet [Matt. 11:9].**

He was a prophet, but he was more than a prophet.

> **For this is he, of whom it is written, Behold, I send my messenger before thy face, which shall prepare thy way before thee [Matt. 11:10].**

The Lord declares clearly that John is the fulfillment of Malachi 3:1, which states: "Behold, I will send my messenger, and he shall prepare the way before me: and the Lord, whom ye seek, shall suddenly come to his temple, even the messenger of the covenant, whom ye delight in: behold, he shall come, saith the LORD of hosts." John was that messenger. John was specially chosen to introduce the Messiah to Israel. Note also John 1:21–23.

> **Verily I say unto you, Among them that are born of women there hath not risen a greater than John the Baptist: notwithstanding he that is least in the kingdom of heaven is greater than he [Matt. 11:11].**

Sometimes we like to debate the question of who was greater: Abraham, Moses, or David. Jesus declares that John is greater than anyone in the past. No one topped John the Baptist.

"Notwithstanding he that is least in the kingdom of heaven is greater than he." When the Lord Jesus came, He began calling out a group of people who are even greater than John the Baptist. How can they be greater? Because they are in Christ and clothed with His righteousness.

> **And from the days of John the Baptist until now the kingdom of heaven suffereth violence, and the violent take it by force [Matt. 11:12].**

This is a difficult verse to interpret because the "force" mentioned can be either internal or external. The forces of evil from without seek to destroy it, that is true. But also those who are committed wholeheartedly press into it; that is, they violently want to come in. There is a note of need and desperation. We have already seen that one young man ran and fell down at Jesus' feet, saying, "Master, I will follow you whithersoever thou goest!" (see Matt. 8:19). There are these two aspects. I am not clear in my own thinking as to what He meant. He may have been referring to both aspects.

For all the prophets and the law prophesied until John.

And if ye will receive it, this is Elias, which was for to come.

He that hath ears to hear, let him hear [Matt. 11:13–15].

John the Baptist fulfilled the prediction of the messenger to come, as recorded in Malachi 3:1. But the question arises: "If Israel had accepted Christ at His first coming, would He have established the kingdom immediately, and would John the Baptist have been Elijah?" The answer is yes. You say, "How can that be?" I have an answer for you: "I don't know." I only know that this is what Jesus said, and He can do things which I cannot explain. In fact, He does a lot of things which I can't explain; I simply accept them.

There are those who argue, "Well, if Christ intended to go to the cross and die, His offer of Himself as King was not a sincere offer." But it *was* sincere. "But," they insist, "what if Israel had accepted Jesus as their King?" Well, the point is that they *didn't!* These are "if" questions we are asking, and the fact is that the Jews rejected the Lord. "Iffy" questions pose problems that don't exist. And there are enough problems that do exist without making up some!

The next two verses compose one of the Lord's parables that was loaded with biting sarcasm and irony. The Lord did not give this story to hurt or to harm but to illustrate a great truth.

But whereunto shall I liken this generation? It is like unto children sitting in the markets, and calling unto their fellows,

And saying, We have piped unto you, and ye have not danced; we have mourned unto you, and ye have not lamented [Matt. 11:16–17].

This is a picture of a group of children out playing in the streets. One group says, "Let's play funeral." They play funeral for awhile, soon tire of it and then say, "Let's play wedding." Soon they grow tired of playing wedding. They go from one extreme to another. They are spoiled children. The generation Jesus was speaking to was like that, and our generation is also.

For John came neither eating nor drinking, and they say, He hath a devil [Matt. 11:18].

John was both austere and severe. And they didn't feel comfortable with him.

The Son of man came eating and drinking, and they say, Behold a man gluttonous, and a winebibber, a friend of publicans and sinners. But wisdom is justified of her children [Matt. 11:19].

Jesus was friendly. What about Him? "Oh, He is gluttonous. He's too friendly with sinners!" They weren't pleased with John, nor were they pleased with Jesus.

There are some folk that you simply cannot please, and you are better off to forget about them. They don't like one preacher because he just stands up there and in a monotone gives his sermon. Then the next preacher they don't like because he is very demonstrative and pounds the pulpit. Or one is too profound, and they don't understand him, and the other is too simple—so they don't like him either. There are a lot of people whom no one can please, and that was certainly true in our Lord's day.

JESUS REJECTS UNREPENTANT CITIES

We have now come to a tremendous change. Remember that Jesus is the King. He has enunciated the ethic, He has presented His credentials by performing miracles, He has preached the gospel that the Kingdom of Heaven is at hand, He has presented Himself, but His people have rejected Him. Their rejection has caused Him to make a decision, and He rejects them. He is the King, and the King always has the last word.

> **Then began he to upbraid the cities wherein most of his mighty works were done, because they repented not:**
>
> **Woe unto thee, Chorazin! woe unto thee, Bethsaida! for if the mighty works, which were done in you, had been done in Tyre and Sidon, they would have repented long ago in sackcloth and ashes [Matt. 11:20–21].**

Chorazin and Bethsaida were cities in the north near Capernaum where the Lord had His headquarters. He had performed many miracles in this area. They rejected Him, and now He pronounces a judgment upon them.

> **But I say unto you, It shall be more tolerable for Tyre and Sidon at the day of judgment, than for you [Matt. 11:22].**

Light creates responsibility. The Lord never had a ministry in Tyre or Sidon, nor did He have His headquarters there. But He spent a lot of time in the area of Chorazin and Bethsaida, and He holds them responsible for the light which He gave them. It is my understanding that there will be degrees of punishment as well as degrees of reward at the time of God's judgment. Even in our own day, there are many folk who have had a glorious opportunity to receive Christ, but they have turned their backs on Him.

Without going into detail, let me say this: I do not know what God will do with that person on a little island in the South Pacific who has never heard the gospel and bows down and worships an image. I do know what God is going to do with that person who comes and sits in church Sunday after Sunday and hears the gospel and does nothing about it.

Now the Lord speaks of Capernaum, His headquarters.

> **And thou, Capernaum, which art exalted unto heaven, shalt be brought down to hell: for if the mighty works, which have been done in thee, had been done in Sodom, it would have remained until this day [Matt. 11:23].**

What a privilege was theirs in having the headquarters of the Lord Jesus in their city! But they rejected Him. The Lord Jesus is saying that if the wicked city of Sodom had witnessed the miracles that He had performed in Capernaum, they would have turned from their wickedness and would not have merited the judgment that came upon them.

> **But I say unto you, That it shall be more tolerable for the land of Sodom in the day of judgment, than for thee [Matt. 11:24].**

This is the harshest language of all. Remember it fell from the lips of the gentle Jesus. He speaks here as the Judge and King. This strong language ought to make us sit up and listen. I would much rather be a Hottentot in the darkness of a jungle without having heard the gospel than to be an officer in one of our modern churches, having a Bible but never truly having accepted Christ as Savior.

Although Sodom and Gomorrah were terrible places, it will be more tolerable for them in the day of judgment than for cities that heard the message of Jesus and rejected Him.

> **At that time Jesus answered and said, I thank thee, O Father, Lord of heaven and earth, because thou hast hid these things from the wise and prudent, and hast revealed them unto babes.**
>
> **Even so, Father: for so it seemed good in thy sight [Matt. 11:25–26].**

The phrase "Lord of heaven" takes you back to Genesis 14:19, where God is called by this name. He is the Lord of heaven and earth. Many wise people never learn this truth, but many babes understand it. Dr. Harry Ironside said many years ago, "Always put the cookies on the bottom shelf so the kiddos can get them." If you preach so children understand what you are saying, you can almost be sure the older folks will understand—but sometimes the children get it and the adults miss it.

> **All things are delivered unto me of my Father: and no man knoweth the Son, but the Father; neither knoweth any man the Father, save the Son, and he to whomsoever the Son will reveal him [Matt. 11:27].**

This is another way of saying, ". . . no man cometh unto the Father, but by me" (John 14:6).

JESUS ISSUES NEW INVITATION TO INDIVIDUALS

These verses bring us to a definite break and change in the Lord's message. Up to this point the Lord taught, "Repent, the kingdom of heaven is at hand." He had presented His credentials and had been rejected as the Messiah. These cities which have been mentioned turned their backs upon Him, and so had Jerusalem. The Lord now turns His back upon the nation Israel, no longer presenting to them the Kingdom. He is on His way to the cross, and His invitation is to the individual. Listen to Him:

> **Come unto me, all ye that labour and are heavy laden, and I will give you rest.**
>
> **Take my yoke upon you, and learn of me; for I am meek and lowly in heart: and ye shall find rest unto your souls.**
>
> **For my yoke is easy, and my burden is light [Matt. 11:28–30].**

This language is in contrast to what has preceded it in this chapter. It is like coming out of a blizzard into the warmth of a spring day, like passing from a storm into a calm, like going from darkness into light. This is a new message from Jesus. He turns from the corporate nation to the individual. It is no longer the national announcement about a kingdom but a personal invitation to find the "rest" of salvation.

"I will give you rest" is literally "I will rest you." When He speaks of being "heavy laden," He is referring to being burdened with sin.

This same figure is used by Isaiah and the psalmist: "Ah sinful nation, a people laden with iniquity, a seed of evildoers, children that are corrupters: they have forsaken the LORD, they have provoked the Holy One of Israel unto anger, they are gone away backward" (Isa. 1:4). "For mine iniquities are gone over mine head: as an heavy burden they are too heavy for me" (Ps. 38:4).

My friend, sin is too heavy for you to carry—you'll really get a hernia if you try to carry your load of sin! The only place in the world to put that burden is at the Cross of Christ. He bore it for you, and He invites you to come and bring your burden of sin to Him. He can forgive you because on the cross He bore the burden of your sin.

"Come unto me, all ye that labour and are heavy laden, and I will give you rest" refers to the salvation of the sinner through Jesus Christ. "Take my yoke upon you, and learn of me; for I am meek and lowly in heart: and ye shall find rest unto your souls" refers to the practical sanctification of the believer. There is a *rest* which Jesus gives, and it is the rest of redemption. There is also a *rest* which the believer experiences, and it comes through commitment and consecration to Christ. You don't have to worry about being recognized; you don't have to jockey for position if you are committed to Christ. Frankly, I quit joining organizations because I got so tired of watching ambitious men trying to be chairman of something or trying to be president of something. If you are committed to Christ, you don't have to worry about that. He will put you exactly where *He* wants you when you are yoked up to Him.

CHAPTER 12

THEME: Conflict and final break of Jesus with the religious rulers

Again let me call your attention to the movement in the Gospel of Matthew. If you miss it, you miss the message that is here. Matthew is not trying to give a biography of the life of Jesus, nor is he recording the events in chronological order. He presents Christ as King—He was born a King and gave what we call the Sermon on the Mount, which was the ethic of the Kingdom, the manifesto of the King. He demonstrated that He had the dynamic in the miracles He performed, then He sent out His apostles. The reaction was rejection! And then the King pronounced judgment on the cities.

Now there breaks out into the open a conflict between the Lord Jesus and the religious rulers of that day—the Pharisees in particular. Apparently, they were friendly to Him at first, but now they break with Him over the question of the Sabbath day.

We will see the Sabbath question in two places: on the outside in the field, then again on the inside in the synagogue.

JESUS CLAIMS TO BE LORD OF THE SABBATH

At that time Jesus went on the sabbath day through the corn; and his disciples were an hungered, and began to pluck the ears of corn, and to eat [Matt. 12:1].

We will see in this episode that Jesus asserts that He is Lord of the Sabbath day. But before we get involved in the sabbatic argument (which has been raging ever since!), let's look at the *reason* the disciples were pulling off and eating the grain. Why were they doing it? Because they were hungry. Why were they hungry? Because they were following Jesus. You remember that He had said to the young man who wanted to follow Him, "The foxes have holes, and the birds of the air have nests; but the Son of man hath not where to lay his head" (Matt. 8:20). And at this time, they were hungry. This is another reminder of the poverty that our Lord bore. And we will see Him defend His disciples' actions. This is where the break with the religious rulers came.

> **But when the Pharisees saw it, they said unto him, Behold, thy disciples do that which is not lawful to do upon the sabbath day [Matt. 12:2].**

The Pharisees say to the Lord Jesus, "Why do You permit it?"

> **But he said unto them, Have ye not read what David did, when he was an hungered, and they that were with him [Matt. 12:3].**

We find the record of this in 1 Samuel 21:1–6. It was during the days of David's rejection as king while Saul was ruling. Likewise, the Lord Jesus was being rejected as King; His messianic claim had not been acknowledged. Now He takes care of His men—regardless of the Sabbath day observance. And David took care of his men although it meant breaking the Mosaic Law.

> **How he entered into the house of God, and did eat the shewbread, which was not lawful for him to eat, neither for them which were with him, but only for the priests?**
>
> **Or have ye not read in the law, how that on the sabbath days the priests in the temple profane the sabbath, and are blameless? [Matt. 12:4–5].**

The priests worked on the Sabbath day.

> **But I say unto you, That in this place is one greater than the temple [Matt. 12:6].**

The Lord Jesus here claimed superiority over the most holy center of their religious life, which was the temple. As far as the Pharisees were concerned, He had blasphemed. Not only had He broken the Sabbath, but He had blasphemed.

> **But if ye had known what this meaneth, I will have mercy, and not sacrifice, ye would not have condemned the guiltless [Matt. 12:7].**

"I will have mercy and not sacrifice" comes from Hosea 6:6. Our Lord defends His men by saying that they did not break the Sabbath day. Why?

> **For the Son of man is Lord even of the sabbath day [Matt. 12:8].**

Believe me, He put His hand on the most sacred observance they had when He said that He was Lord of the Sabbath day. In the eyes of the Pharisees, He could make no greater claim. It certainly engendered their bitterness and their hatred.

Now we leave the fields where this encounter took place, and we go into the synagogue—but we are still faced with the same Sabbath question.

> **And when he was departed thence, he went into their synagogue [Matt. 12:9].**

Notice that "he went into their synagogue"—not *ours* but *theirs*. He said something similar regarding the temple. At first it was *God's* temple, but He finally said, "*Your* house is left unto you desolate."

> **And, behold, there was a man which had his hand withered. And they asked him, saying, Is it lawful to heal on the sabbath days? that they might accuse him.**

And he said unto them, What man shall there be among you, that shall have one sheep, and if it fall into a pit on the sabbath day, will he not lay hold on it, and lift it out? [Matt. 12:10–11].

Was this man with the withered hand "planted" there, deliberately, by the Pharisees to trap Jesus into healing him? If so, then there are two important admissions on the part of the enemies of Jesus:

1. They admitted He had power to heal the sick. As we have seen, the enemies of Jesus never questioned His ability to perform miracles. You have to be two thousand years away from it and working in a musty library on a master's or doctor's degree before you can question His miracles. The Pharisees freely admitted that He had power to heal the sick. This is why they planted this man with the withered hand.

2. They acknowledged that when a helpless man was placed in His pathway, He was moved by compassion to heal him, even on the Sabbath day. What an admission!

Their question about the legality of healing on the Sabbath day was designed to trap Him. But Jesus actually trapped His enemies. They conceded that a sheep should be rescued on the Sabbath day—in fact, the Mosaic Law made allowances for that.

How much then is a man better than a sheep? Wherefore it is lawful to do well on the sabbath days [Matt. 12:12].

This is the crux of the whole matter: Should He do good on the Sabbath day? Regardless of their answer—

Then saith he to the man, Stretch forth thine hand. And he stretched it forth; and it was restored whole, like as the other [Matt. 12:13].

Jesus healed the man on the Sabbath day. Did He break the Law? What is your answer? My answer is that He did *not* break the Law.

THE PHARISEES PLOT THE DEATH OF JESUS

This marks the break between the religious rulers and Jesus. Here is where they made the decision to destroy Him.

Then the Pharisees went out, and held a council against him, how they might destroy him [Matt. 12:14].

Up to this point the Pharisees had been friendly. They had wanted to hitch their wagon to His star and go with Him. But the Lord refused to go along with them, and they became His enemies. The break is made over the question of the Sabbath day, and the conflict comes out in the open. From here on these bloodhounds of hate get on His trail and never let up until they fold their arms beneath His cross. They begin now to plot His death, and they undoubtedly want to arrest Him at this time, but they are afraid of the crowds.

But when Jesus knew it, he withdrew himself from thence: and great multitudes followed him, and he healed them all [Matt. 12:15].

The action of the Pharisees led Jesus to withdraw temporarily because His hour had not yet come. They will not touch Him until the appointed time. It is interesting to note in this verse that Jesus did not heal only a few in the crowd—He healed them *all*. We cannot even conceive of the impression that this made in that day. It was something absolutely astounding. They had to accept or reject Him; it was impossible to be neutral.

He is still controversial today. The enemy is still after Him. New dirty plays and dirty books are blaspheming Him. You will either be His friend or His enemy. He will be your Savior or your Judge. You cannot get rid of Jesus Christ.

He healed the multitudes—

And charged them that they should not make him known [Matt. 12:16].

The Lord did not come to this earth as a thaumaturgist, that is, a wonder worker. He came to present His claims as Messiah. When He was rejected, He continued on His course toward the cross to become the Savior of the world. His miracles caused crowds to press in upon Him so that He could not carry on His ministry as He wished.

> **That it might be fulfilled which was spoken by Esaias the prophet, saying,**
>
> **Behold my servant, whom I have chosen; my beloved, in whom my soul is well pleased: I will put my spirit upon him, and he shall shew judgment to the Gentiles.**
>
> **He shall not strive, nor cry; neither shall any man hear his voice in the streets.**
>
> **A bruised reed shall he not break, and smoking flax shall he not quench, till he send forth judgment unto victory [Matt. 12:17–20].**

"A bruised reed shall he not break"—no, He will instead bind up that "reed" who will let Him do so. "And smoking flax shall he not quench"—no, if that one continues to reject Him, the smoking flax will break out into the fire of judgment. The Lord won't quench it because man has a free will.

And in his name shall the Gentiles trust [Matt. 12:21].

In our day, friend, there is a definite moving out—not only toward the fulfillment of prophecy in general, but for the fulfillment of prophecy concerning the Gentiles. They are to be saved. Christ's rejection by His own people led to His gracious offer to the Gentiles. In the Book of Acts we read that He commissioned Paul to be a missionary to the Gentiles: "To open their eyes, and to turn them from darkness to light, and from the power of Satan unto God, that they may receive forgiveness of sins, and inheritance among them which are sanctified by faith that is in me" (Acts 26:18).

THE UNPARDONABLE SIN

Then was brought unto him one possessed with a devil, blind, and dumb: and he healed him, insomuch that the blind and dumb both spake and saw.

And all the people were amazed, and said, Is not this the son of David? [Matt. 12:22–23].

In other words, "This is our Messiah. He has the credentials." This was a tremendous miracle He performed, just as great as the raising of the dead if not greater. The continued miracles of Jesus in healing and casting out demons convinced the people that He was the Son of David, the Messiah. But what did the Pharisees say?

But when the Pharisees heard it, they said, This fellow doth not cast out devils, but by Beelzebub the prince of the devils [Matt. 12:24].

This is the question of the unpardonable sin. Follow this very carefully.

And Jesus knew their thoughts, and said unto them, Every kingdom divided against itself is brought to desolation; and every city or house divided against itself shall not stand:

And if Satan cast out Satan, he is divided against himself; how shall then his kingdom stand?

And if I by Beelzebub cast out devils, by whom do your children cast them out? therefore they shall be your judges [Matt. 12:25–27].

They would never say that their own people cast out demons by Beelzebub.

But if I cast out devils by the Spirit of God, then the kingdom of God is come unto you [Matt. 12:28].

"The kingdom of God is come unto you" in the presence of the Messiah. Christ is saying, "I am here! My power to cast out demons is My credential."

Or else how can one enter into a strong man's house, and spoil his goods, except he first bind the strong man? and then he will spoil his house.

He that is not with me is against me; and he that gathereth not with me scattereth abroad.

Wherefore I say unto you, All manner of sin and blasphemy shall be forgiven unto men: but the blasphemy against the Holy Ghost shall not be forgiven unto men.

And whosoever speaketh a word against the Son of man, it shall be forgiven him: but whosoever speaketh against the Holy Ghost, it shall not be forgiven him, neither in this world, neither in the world to come [Matt. 12:29–32].

There is no sin committed yesterday that the Lord would not forgive today because He died for *all* sin. The Holy Spirit came into the world to make real the salvation of Christ to the hearts of men. If you resist the working of the Spirit of God when He speaks to you, my friend, there is no forgiveness, of course. There is no forgiveness because you have rejected salvation made real to you by the Holy Spirit. And it is the work of the Spirit of God to regenerate you.

In Mark 3 the Lord amplifies the matter of the unpardonable sin by saying that it attributes the Spirit's work to Satan, that Christ had performed these miracles by Beelzebub when actually He was doing them by the power of the Spirit of God. You see, they were rejecting the witness of Himself and of the Holy Spirit.

In our day that particular sin cannot be committed because it could only be committed when Jesus was here upon the earth. There is no act of sin that you could commit for which there is no forgiveness. Of course, if you resist the Holy Spirit, there is no forgiveness because He is bringing forgiveness. It is like the man who is dying from a certain disease, and the doctor tells him there is a remedy for it. The man refuses to take the remedy and dies, not from the disease but from refusing to take the remedy. There is a remedy for the disease of sin, and the Holy Spirit applies it; but if you resist it, there is no remedy. That is the only way sin can be unpardonable today.

Now the Lord says:

O generation of vipers, how can ye, being evil, speak good things? for out of the abundance of the heart the mouth speaketh [Matt. 12:34].

"O generation of vipers"—you may remember that John the Baptist had called them the same thing.

A good man out of the good treasure of the heart bringeth forth good things: and an evil man out of the evil treasure bringeth forth evil things [Matt. 12:35].

"What is in the well of the heart will come out through the bucket of the mouth," someone has said. This scathing denunciation of the religious rulers by Jesus reveals that He has rejected them. Had they committed the unpardonable sin? At least the break with these enemies is final and the wound will not be healed.

But I say unto you, That every idle word that men shall speak, they shall give account thereof in the day of judgment [Matt. 12:36].

"Idle word" means blasphemies.

For by thy words thou shalt be justified, and by thy words thou shalt be condemned [Matt. 12:37].

You will be "condemned" because you are speaking the thing which is in your heart.

THE SCRIBES AND PHARISEES DEMAND A SIGN

Then certain of the scribes and of the Pharisees answered, saying, Master, we would see a sign from thee [Matt. 12:38].

The scribes and Pharisees now use another subtle approach to Him. They appear to fall in step with His program by asking for a sign. They have no intention of believing because of a sign. They are trying to trap Him. Note how the Lord answers them.

But he answered and said unto them, An evil and adulterous generation seeketh after a sign; and there shall no sign be given to it, but the sign of the prophet Jonas [Matt. 12:39].

What was the sign of Jonah? Well, listen to Him—

For as Jonas was three days and three nights in the whale's belly; so shall the Son of man be three days and three nights in the heart of the earth [Matt. 12:40].

The Lord categorically refused to grant them a sign but directed them back to two incidents in the Old Testament. The first incident is the account of the prophet Jonah. Jonah was apparently raised from the dead when he was in the fish. God brought him out of darkness and death into light and life. Jonah's experience was typical of the coming interment and resurrection of Jesus Christ.

The men of Nineveh shall rise in judgment with this generation, and shall condemn it: because they repented at the preaching of Jonas; and, behold, a greater than Jonas is here [Matt. 12:41].

The Ninevites received Jonah and his preaching after his miraculous deliverance from the big fish, and they repented. The acts of Israel, as a nation, place her in a much worse position because she did not receive her Messiah and did not repent.

The second incident that Jesus referred them to concerns Solomon.

> **The queen of the south shall rise up in the judgment with this generation, and shall condemn it: for she came from the uttermost parts of the earth to hear the wisdom of Solomon; and, behold, a greater than Solomon is here [Matt. 12:42].**

Jesus was greater than Jonah and greater than Solomon. The queen of Sheba heard of Solomon and traveled from the ends of the earth to hear his wisdom. And the Lord Jesus Christ had come from heaven, but they would not turn to Him.

VALUELESS REFORMATION

Next Jesus gives one of the most profound and startling parables.

> **When the unclean spirit is gone out of a man, he walketh through dry places, seeking rest, and findeth none [Matt. 12:43].**

A man has an unclean spirit, and the unclean spirit leaves him. The man thinks he is all cleaned up. Then what happens?

> **Then he saith, I will return into my house from whence I came out; and when he is come, he findeth it empty, swept, and garnished [Matt. 12:44].**

In other words, reformation is no good. My friend, you can quit doing many things, but that won't make you a Christian. If everyone in the world would quit sinning right now, there wouldn't be any more

Christians in the next minute or in the next day, because quitting sin doesn't make Christians. Reformation is not what we need.

> **Then goeth he, and taketh with himself seven other spirits more wicked than himself, and they enter in and dwell there: and the last state of that man is worse than the first. Even so shall it be also unto this wicked generation [Matt. 12:45].**

This same situation is with us today. The hardest people in the world are unsaved church members because they think they are all right. They have undergone self-reformation—empty, swept, and garnished. They are like a vacant house, and all the evil spirits have to do is move in. The Devil owns them, and they don't recognize this fact. Reformation means death and destruction. Regeneration means life and liberty.

The final section of this chapter is even more startling, and it belongs with what has immediately preceded. There is a relationship that is greater than mother and son and even blood brothers! This is a relationship which is established with God through Jesus Christ by faith in Him.

> **While he yet talked to the people, behold, his mother and his brethren stood without, desiring to speak with him.**
>
> **Then one said unto him, Behold, thy mother and thy brethren stand without, desiring to speak with thee.**
>
> **But he answered and said unto him that told him, Who is my mother? and who are my brethren?**
>
> **And he stretched forth his hand toward his disciples, and said, Behold my mother and my brethren! [Matt. 12:46–49].**

The Lord is saying that the strongest relationship today is the relationship between Christ and a believer. Friend, if you are a child of God and you have unsaved family members, you are closer to Jesus Christ than you are to your own kin, including the mother that bore you. You are more closely related to other believers than you are to unsaved members of your family. This is tremendous! He is talking about a new relationship.

> **For whosoever shall do the will of my Father which is in heaven, the same is my brother, and sister, and mother [Matt. 12:50].**

And what is the will of the Father? That you hear the Lord Jesus Christ, that you accept Him and trust Him.

CHAPTER 13

THEME: The parables of the Kingdom of Heaven show the direction of the Kingdom after Israel's rejection of it until the King returns to establish the Kingdom of Heaven on the earth

As we have said, the Gospel of Matthew is probably the key Gospel to the Bible. It is the open door to both the Old and the New Testaments. If that is true, then chapter 13 is the key to the Gospel of Matthew. This makes chapter 13 all-important. It will give us a better understanding of what the Kingdom of Heaven is than any other place in the Book. We call it the Mystery Parables Discourse, and it is one of the three major discourses in the Gospel of Matthew.

1. The Sermon on the Mount looks back to the past. It is the law for the land.

2. The Mystery Parables Discourse reveals the condition of the Kingdom of Heaven in the world during the present age.

3. The Olivet Discourse looks to the future, to the return of the King and the things beyond this age.

Let me remind you that our Lord followed John the Baptist in preaching, ". . . Repent: for the kingdom of heaven is at hand" (Matt. 4:17). And our Lord enunciated the law of that Kingdom, the Sermon on the Mount. Then He demonstrated that He had the power, the dynamic, after which He sent His disciples out with the message. The message was met by rejection—Israel rejected its King. Therefore, our Lord hands down a judgment against the cities where His mighty works had been done and against the religious rulers. When they asked Him for a sign, He said that no sign would be given to them except that of Jonah. Jonah was a resurrection sign, and they were to have that fulfilled in Christ shortly after this. Finally, He gave that very personal invitation, "Come unto me, all ye that labour and are heavy laden, and I will give you rest (lit., "rest you")" (Matt. 11:28).

Now the question arises: What will happen to the Kingdom of Heaven? It is apparent that He will not establish it on the earth at His first coming. So what will happen to the Kingdom of Heaven during the interval between the suffering and the glory of Christ? Well, in the Mystery Parables Discourse our Lord sets before us Kingdom-of-Heaven conditions on earth during this interval, using seven or eight parables.

We call them Mystery Parables because in the Word of God a mystery is something hidden or secret up to a certain time and then revealed. The church is a mystery (according to this definition) since it was not a matter of revelation in the Old Testament. It was revealed after the death and resurrection of Christ. Actually, there could be no church until Christ died and rose again. Ephesians 5:25 says that ". . . Christ also loved the church, and gave himself for it."

It is important to note that the Kingdom of Heaven is not synonymous with the church nor is the church synonymous with the Kingdom of Heaven. The Kingdom of Heaven today is all Christendom (the portion of the world in which Christianity is predominant can be considered as Christendom). Obviously, the church is in Christendom, but it is not all of it by any means.

These Mystery Parables show the direction of the Kingdom after it had been offered and rejected by Israel. They reveal what is going to take place between the time of Christ's rejection and the time when He returns to the earth as King. With these parables our Lord covers the entire period between His rejection by Israel and His return to the earth to establish His Kingdom. I consider them very important.

As we begin this chapter, notice that the very actions of Jesus are interesting.

The same day went Jesus out of the house, and sat by the sea side.

And great multitudes were gathered together unto him, so that he went into a ship, and sat; and the whole multitude stood on the shore [Matt. 13:1–2].

Notice the symbolism here. "The same day went Jesus out of the house," which speaks of the house of Israel. "And sat by the sea side"—the sea represents the gentile nations (a symbolism used elsewhere in Scripture). Our Lord is leaving the nation of Israel and turning to the world. He is now speaking of what will take place in the world until He returns as King.

This act denotes a tremendous change that has taken place in His method. Great multitudes were gathered together to hear Him, and He went into a ship and began to talk to them as they stood on the shore.

PARABLE OF THE SOWER

Although our Lord gives several parables in this chapter, He interprets only two of them: the parable of the sower and the parable of the wheat and tares. His interpretation is a guide to the symbolism in the other parables. For instance, in this parable of the sower, the birds represent Satan. Now when He uses the symbol of birds in another parable, we may be sure that they do not represent something good. We need to be consistent and follow our Lord's interpretation.

The parable of the sower is the first of the Mystery Parables and may be considered as the foundation for all of them.

And he spake many things unto them in parables, saying, Behold, a sower went forth to sow [Matt. 13:3].

I'll just run ahead and give you our Lord's interpretation of the sower. He will tell us later that the sower is the Son of man and that the seed represents the Word of God.

And when he sowed, some seeds fell by the way side, and the fowls came and devoured them up:

Some fell upon stony places, where they had not much earth: and forthwith they sprung up, because they had no deepness of earth:

> **And when the sun was up, they were scorched; and because they had no root, they withered away.**
>
> **And some fell among thorns; and the thorns sprung up, and choked them:**
>
> **But other fell into good ground, and brought forth fruit, some an hundredfold, some sixtyfold, some thirtyfold [Matt. 13:4–8].**

Sowing seed was a familiar sight in Palestine. They would sort of scratch the surface of the ground with a very crude plow. Sometimes they didn't even do that much. Then the sower would go out and fling the seeds upon the earth. Even today in our land in the springtime, all the way from Pocatello, Idaho, to Pensacola, Florida, and from Minnesota to Muleshoe, Texas, you will see farmers sowing wheat, corn, and cotton. It is a very familiar sight—of course, *we* use machines to sow the seed, while in that day it was sown by hand.

As I have mentioned, the sower represents the Lord Jesus—we learn this from the parable of the wheat and tares (v. 37). The Lord Jesus is the One sowing the seed, and I feel that this defines His work today in the world. He was the King, but He laid aside His regal robes, and today He is doing the work of a farmer, sowing seed—but He is still the King.

The *seed*, we learn from verse 19, represents the Word of God. The *field* symbolizes the world (v. 38). Notice that it is the world, not the church. We are talking about a world situation. I think the picture is something like this: Here is the church in the world, and outside there are multitudes of people who have not received Christ. The Word of God is given to this one, and the Word is given to that one, and the Word is given to another. One accepts, another does not accept. Our business is to sow the seed, although not everyone will receive it.

The Lord Jesus has charge of this great program of sowing seed. He has given me a little corner to work in, and my business is to sow seed. I want to be specific here. This is the day for sowing seed. I don't want to split hairs, but the "harvest" is *not* the picture for today. But someone says, "Didn't Christ say, 'Pray ye therefore the Lord of the harvest'?" Yes, and let's look at it again: "But when he saw the multitudes, he was moved with compassion on them, because they fainted, and were scattered abroad, as sheep having no shepherd. Then saith he unto his disciples, The harvest truly is plenteous, but the labourers are few; pray ye therefore the Lord of the harvest, that he will send forth labourers into his harvest" (Matt. 9:36–38).

This passage occurs just before the Lord sent out His apostles to the lost sheep of the house of Israel. The age of the Law was coming to an end. Harvest time comes *after* seed has been sown. For fifteen hundred years, approximately, under Law, the seed had been sown. Then the harvest came, and a new age, a new dispensation, came in. At the close of one age there is a harvest, and at the beginning of another age is the sowing of seed. But I want to emphasize that the harvest at the end of an age is *judgment*. We will see that in some of the parables which follow.

However, in our day we are to be sowing the seed of the Word of God. I rejoice when I receive a letter from someone who has listened to my teaching of the Word by radio. Some folk listen for a year or more, and finally the seed germinates and brings forth fruit. It is my business to sow the seed while I am in the world, and it is your business also, my friend.

Now notice where the seed falls. It falls on four types of soil, and three-fourths of the seeds do not grow—they die. There was nothing wrong with the seed, but the soil was the problem. You can argue election all you want to, but in this parable there is a lot of free will exhibited. The condition of the soil is all important as far as the seed is concerned.

Now let's look at our Lord's interpretation of the types of soil on which the seed fell. In verse 4 He says that some of it fell by the wayside, and the birds came and ate it up. In verse 19 He explains to His disciples the meaning of it—

When any one heareth the word of the kingdom, and understandeth it not, then cometh the wicked one, and catcheth away that which was sown in his heart. This is he which received seed by the way side [Matt. 13:19].

The birds represent the evil one—the Devil takes away the seed sown by the wayside. This is something which ought to cause every church member to examine his own heart. My friend, don't apply this to the other fellow, apply it to yourself. Someone has written a clever little poem which says:

> When you get to heaven
> You will likely view,
> Many folk there
> Who'll be a shock to you.
>
> But don't act surprised,
> Or even show a care,
> For they might be a little shocked
> To see you there.

The wayside soil apparently represents church members, professing Christians. They heard the Word of God, but it was not the hearing of faith. The Word was not mixed with faith—or if it was, it was a formal, intellectual faith which simply nodded the head. In other words, to folk like this, Christianity is a sideline. Belonging to the church is like belonging to a lodge or a club. These folk are in deep freeze. Not only do we find them in our churches, but some of them have fallen away from the church and are in cults and "isms."

The second group are represented by the rocky soil.

But he that received the seed into stony places, the same is he that heareth the word, and anon with joy receiveth it;

Yet hath he not root in himself, but dureth for a while: for when tribulation or persecution ariseth because of the word, by and by he is offended [Matt. 13:20–21].

These rocky-ground folk are the opposite of the first group. It was the Devil who took the Word away from the wayside hearers, but the flesh is the culprit with this group. Instead of being in deep freeze, they are in the oven—warm, emotional, shedding tears, greatly moved. These are what I call Alka-Seltzer Christians. There is a lot of fizz in them. They make as much fuss during a service as a rocket on a launching pad, but they never get into orbit. I classify them as the Southern California type. They have great zeal and energy during special meetings, but they are like burned out Roman candles after the meetings are over.

I stood on the rear end of a train, years ago, going through Kansas. Someone had thrown a paper onto the railroad tracks. As our train sped past, the paper fluttered up into the air and went in every direction. As soon as the train had gone by, the paper settled down on the track and was soon dead still. As I looked way back at the paper lying there, I thought, "That is just like a lot of so-called Christians. When there is a sensational meeting in progress, they really get enthusiastic, but they have no real relationship with Christ. It is just an emotional high." They are the rocky-ground folk.

The third group of hearers is like thorny ground—

> **He also that received seed among the thorns is he that heareth the word; and the care of this world, and the deceitfulness of riches, choke the word, and he becometh unfruitful [Matt. 13:22].**

With these folk the world crowds out the Word of God. The Devil got the wayside folk, and the flesh took care of the rocky-ground folk, but the world chokes out the Word for this class of hearers. The cares of the world move in. Sometimes it is poverty, and other times it is the deceitfulness of riches. It is quite interesting that folk at each end of the social spectrum—extreme poverty and extreme prosperity—are folk who are the most difficult to reach for Christ. I find that a great many people have let the cares of the world crowd out the Word of God. These three types of soil do not represent three types of believers—they are not believers at all! They have heard the Word and have only professed to receive it. My friend, it is well for all of us to examine ourselves to see whether or not we are really in the faith.

Thank God, some seed falls on good ground, and our Lord interprets this for us—

> **But he that received seed into the good ground is he that heareth the word, and understandeth it; which also beareth fruit, and bringeth forth, some an hundredfold, some sixty, some thirty [Matt. 13:23].**

These are the hearers who receive the Word and understand it. Some of them don't bring forth much fruit—only thirtyfold, but some bring forth an hundredfold!

There must be an understanding of the Word. The Ethiopian eunuch, you remember, was reading the Word, but he didn't understand it—although he *wanted* to understand it. So the Spirit of God put Philip there as a hitchhiker. He took a ride with the Ethiopian and gave him a ticket to heaven. He explained the Word to him—that the One who was led as a sheep to the slaughter was the Lord Jesus Christ, that He was wounded for our transgressions and bruised for our iniquities. The Ethiopian believed and received Him.

Philip was sowing the seed of the Word of God. This is a Kingdom-of-Heaven situation as it reveals that the Sower, the Lord Jesus Christ, is sowing the seed of the Word of God in the world and that the Holy Spirit applies it to the hearts of those who want to believe.

After our Lord had given the parable of the sower, He said something quite interesting—

> **Who hath ears to hear, let him hear [Matt. 13:9].**

Well, if we have these things on the side of our head called ears, can't we hear Him? Yes, but notice the question and His answer—

> **And the disciples came, and said unto him, Why speakest thou unto them in parables? [Matt. 13:10].**

Someone has said that a parable is an earthly story with a heavenly meaning. This is a good definition. But the word *parable* is from the Greek *parabolē*. We get our English word *ball* from it. You throw something down beside an object to measure it. For example, it's like putting a ruler down beside a table to measure it. That ruler is a parable; it is put down for the purpose of measuring. Our Lord gave parables to measure heavenly truth which He could set before us.

Why did He do it?

He answered and said unto them, Because it is given unto you to know the mysteries of the kingdom of heaven, but to them it is not given [Matt. 13:11].

If a man *wants* to know the Word of God, he can know it. He who wants to know the truth can know it. But you can shut your ears to it. There are multitudes of so-called broadminded people who shut their ears to the Word of God. If you don't want to hear it, you won't hear it, my friend. Not only would you fail to hear it, but you wouldn't understand it if you did hear it. You must have the kind of ear that wants to hear the Word of God.

For whosoever hath, to him shall be given, and he shall have more abundance: but whosoever hath not, from him shall be taken away even that he hath [Matt. 13:12].

If you know a little truth and you want to know more, the Lord will add to it. If you don't want to know the truth, the Lord will see to it that you won't get it. You see, the Lord will never shut the door to one who wants to hear. He makes it very clear that this is His reason for speaking in parables. Those who don't want to hear will not understand them.

The Lord drew His parables from commonplace things, things that were at the fingertips of the people in that day. He gave them great spiritual truths illustrated by things they knew and could see. Someone has put this concept in verse—

> He talked of grass and wind and rain
> And fig trees and fair weather,
> And made it His delight to bring
> Heaven and earth together.
>
> He spoke of lilies, vines and corn,
> The sparrow and the raven.
> And words so natural, yet so wise
> Were on men's hearts engraven.

In the parable of the sower, we see what could be called a Kingdom-of-Heaven condition; that is, it exhibits God's present rulership over the entire earth as He calls out a people to His name. And God is carrying out His program today through the church, the called-out body, composed of every true believer. Therefore, we have a Kingdom-of-Heaven condition today as God is carrying on His program of bringing folk to a saving knowledge of Christ.

THE PARABLE OF THE TARES

Another parable put he forth unto them, saying, The kingdom of heaven is likened unto a man which sowed good seed in his field [Matt. 13:24].

In this parable our Lord picks up where He left off in the parable of the sower. He has told us that only one-fourth of the sown seed ever got into good ground. The other three-fourths never did produce anything because the folk who heard the Word did not respond to it. In other words, they were not saved. Of the people who heard the Word of God, only one-fourth were truly saved. Frankly, in my own ministry I have found the percentage even lower than that. If one out of ten responding to my invitation to receive Christ is genuine, I feel that my batting average is good. Other Christian workers tell me the same story. A member of the team of a very prominent evangelist has told me that only three percent of their inquirers can be considered genuine converts. So you see, our batting average is not too good, but we thank God for each person who does come to Christ. We are in a Kingdom-of-Heaven situation, giving out the Word of God—and this is what happens to it.

But now we see another facet of the Kingdom-of-Heaven condition in the world today. It is a picture of a man who sowed good seed in his field—

But while men slept, his enemy came and sowed tares among the wheat, and went his way [Matt. 13:25].

Notice *who* is asleep. While *men* slept, the enemy came. Remember, the sower is the Lord, and He neither slumbers nor sleeps. Satan is the enemy, and he sows tares among the wheat. The tares are false doctrine. There's a great deal of that type of sowing today.

But when the blade was sprung up, and brought forth fruit, then appeared the tares also [Matt. 13:26].

As wheat and tares first begin to grow, it is difficult to distinguish between them. Frankly, a lot of cults and "ism" also sound good at first. You cannot tell them from the real thing until about the twelfth or thirteenth lesson. Those are the lessons in which they introduce their false doctrine. Someone once said to me, "Dr. McGee, you should not criticize so-and-so. I listened to him, and he preached the gospel." Well, he does preach the gospel every now and then. But it is the other things he says that are in error. You see, he sows tares among the wheat.

Now we will see that the sower knew who was responsible for the tares—

So the servants of the householder came and said unto him, Sir, didst not thou sow good seed in thy field? from whence then hath it tares?

He said unto them, An enemy hath done this. The servants said unto him, Wilt thou then that we go and gather them up?

But he said, Nay; lest while ye gather up the tares, ye root up also the wheat with them.

Let both grow together until the harvest: and in the time of harvest I will say to the reapers, Gather ye together first the tares, and bind them in bundles to burn them: but gather the wheat into my barn [Matt. 13:27–30].

This is a very important picture to see and to interpret. Our Lord says, "Don't try to pull up the tares. Let them both grow together, and when they finally head up, you will be able to recognize which are tares and which are wheat."

Somebody comes to me and says, "Pastor McGee, do you think the world is getting better?" I reply that I do think it is getting better. Someone else asks me, "Do you think the world is getting worse?" I tell him that I do believe the world is getting worse. A third party who heard me give both answers, says, "What are you trying to do—ride the fence? It is not like you to try to please everybody." Right! But actually, both are true. The wheat is growing and the tares are growing. The world is getting better—the wheat is heading up. Never has there been so much Bible teaching as there is today. I thank God for that. And there are many wonderful saints of God who love His Word and who would die defending it. That wheat is growing, my friend!

However, the world is also getting worse. There are a lot of tares growing. I have been a pastor for a long time. When I began my ministry, I entered a denomination with the idea of cleaning it up. I was the one that just about got cleaned out. I found I could not straighten out my denomination. I was thankful to find out from this passage, and related passages, that my business was to preach the Word. I don't go around pulling up tares anymore because I found that when you pull up tares, you also pull up some wheat with them. But now I know that my business is not to pull up tares but to sow the wheat. Sowing the Word of God is my responsibility.

Both tares and wheat are growing in this world. This is a Kingdom-of-Heaven situation in Christendom during this interval between Christ's rejection and His return to establish His Kingdom upon the earth. It is not a picture of Christ's church. "Well," you say, "it certainly is a picture of the organized church." That is true, but the organized church is not *His* church. His church is composed of that invisible number of saints. When I say invisible, I mean that they are not confined to an organization. (Actually, I do not like the term *invisible* because I find out that a lot of the saints think it means that they are to be invisible Sunday night and at the midweek service. In fact, they are invisible many times.) The true church is made up of true believers, irrespective of any denomination. True believers are those who have trusted Christ as Savior, are resting in Him, and love His Word—this is the real test. Don't be disturbed that the wheat and tares are growing together. One day the Lord will put in His sickle and separate the tares and wheat. I am thankful it will not be my job because I am afraid I would pull up some of the wheat.

THE PARABLE OF THE MUSTARD SEED

This parable presents a different kind of seed.

Another parable put he forth unto them, saying, The kingdom of heaven is like to a grain of mustard seed, which a man took, and sowed in his field:

Which indeed is the least of all seeds: but when it is grown, it is the greatest among herbs, and becometh a tree, so that the birds of the air come and lodge in the branches thereof [Matt. 13:31–32].

The mustard tree is an unlikely symbol of the church or of individual Christians. Ordinarily, fruit-bearing trees are used to depict believers. Mustard is a condiment and has no food value. It's not wheat germ, loaded with vitamins; it's just good on hot dogs and hamburgers. Mustard is not a food you can live on.

The mustard seed does not grow into a mighty oak like the little acorn does. It is a shrub which thrives best in desert lands.

The mustard seed "is the least of all seeds." Several years ago a liberal preacher in our area made the discovery that the mustard seed is not the least of all seeds. He thought he had found an error in the Bible. What did our Lord mean by "the least of all seeds"? It was the least of all seeds that the people in His audience knew about. It is my understanding that it is least of all the seeds in the category of plants to which the mustard belongs. It is a very small seed.

"But when it is grown, it is the greatest among herbs, and becometh a tree, so that the birds of the air come and lodge in the branches thereof." This little seed, which should have become an herb, got to the fertilizer and became a tree large enough for birds to roost in.

This parable reveals the *outward* growth of Christendom as the parable of the leaven speaks of the *internal* condition of Christendom. The church has not converted the world, but it has had a tremendous influence on the world. Any place that Christianity has gone can be called Christendom.

This parable reveals the outward growth of the organized church. The church and the world have become horribly mixed. There has been real integration between man in the church and man in the world. They live and act very much alike in our day. The Christian should be *salt* in the world, not *mustard!*

"The birds of the air come and lodge in the branches thereof." Years ago I heard another liberal preacher interpret the birds as being different denominations. He spoke of the Baptist birds, the Presbyterian birds, the Methodist birds, and all other church groups as being birds. That, of course, is a contradiction of our Lord's own interpretation of the birds in the first parable. We can be sure that the birds in the parables of this discourse do not speak of anything good, but rather they represent evil. The birds are the ones that took the seed which fell by the wayside. Our Lord said that they represent the enemy who is Satan. I am afraid that Christendom today is a mustard tree filled with a lot of dirty birds!

THE PARABLE OF THE LEAVEN

The parable of the leaven is the key parable of this chapter. Let me try to help you realize the importance of it. First of all, the Gospel of

Matthew is the key book of the Bible. Secondly, chapter 13 is the key chapter of Matthew. And thirdly, verse 33 is the key verse of chapter 13. So actually, what we have here is one of the key verses of the Bible! Now notice the very important teaching in this verse—

Another parable spake he unto them; The kingdom of heaven is like unto leaven, which a woman took, and hid in three measures of meal, till the whole was leavened [Matt. 13:33].

"The kingdom of heaven is like unto leaven"—but don't stop there— "which a woman took, and hid in three measures of meal." What does the leaven represent? There are those who interpret the leaven as the gospel, and they ought to know better! Nowhere is leaven used as a principle of good; it is always a principle of evil. The word *leaven* occurs ninety-eight times in the Bible—about seventy-five times in the Old Testament and about twenty-three times in the New Testament—and it is always used in a bad sense. The great scholar, Dr. Lightfoot, made the statement that rabbinical writers regularly used leaven as a symbol of evil. In the Old Testament it was forbidden to be used in the offerings made to God. In the New Testament our Lord warned to beware of the leaven of the Pharisees and of the Sadducees (see Matt. 16:6). And the apostle Paul spoke of the leaven of malice and wickedness (see 1 Cor. 5:8). Symbolism in Scripture does not contradict itself, and we may be certain that leaven is not used in a good sense here in Matthew 13. Leaven is not the gospel.

The gospel is represented by the three measures of meal. How do we know this? Because meal is made out of grain or seed, and our Lord has already told us in the parable of the sower that the seed represents the Word of God.

Remember that this parable is a picture of what happens to the Word of God on this earth during the interval between Christ's rejection and His exaltation when He will return to set up His Kingdom. Note what happens to the Word of God represented by the meal. This woman comes along—I hope you ladies will forgive me for pointing this out—and when a woman is used in a doctrinal sense in Scripture, she is always used as a principle of *evil*. She takes the leaven and hides it in the meal. If the leaven represents the gospel, why in the world did she hide it? The gospel is to be shouted from the housetops and heralded to the very ends of the earth. Obviously, the leaven is a principle of evil, and the woman puts it in the meal, which represents the gospel, the Word of God.

We certainly see this in reality in our day. There is no cult or "ism" which ignores the Bible. I find that even those who worship the Devil, the demon worshipers, use the Bible. False teachers of every description put leaven in the meal, the Word of God.

What does leaven do? Well, leaven is a substance, such as yeast, used to produce fermentation. When it is put in bread dough, it causes it to rise. And it makes it tasty also. That is the reason a great many people find a thrill in some of the cults. Unleavened bread is just blah as far as the natural taste is concerned. A little leaven really helps it. I grew up in the South, and my mother used to make delicious biscuits. She would put leaven in the dough and put them on the back of the stove to rise. If I came running into the kitchen, she would shush me because she didn't want those biscuits to fall. When they got to a certain height, she would stop the fermentation by putting them in the oven and baking them. Have you ever seen what happens when you let dough continue to rise? I tell you, it makes a pan of corruption— something you wouldn't want to eat! Leaven is a principle of evil.

This parable teaches that the intrusion of wrong doctrine into the church will finally lead to total apostasy—"The kingdom of heaven is like unto leaven, which a woman took, and hid in three measures of meal, *till the whole was leavened.*" The Lord Jesus Christ Himself said, ". . . when the Son of man cometh, shall he find faith on the earth?" (Luke 18:8). The way the question is couched in the Greek, it demands a negative answer. In other words, he is saying that when He does return the world will be in total apostasy. And the apostle Paul, writing to a young man studying for the ministry, warns that the time will come when they will not endure sound doctrine (see 2 Tim. 4:3). The final, total apostasy of the church is revealed in the church of Laodicea (see Rev. 3:14–19).

> All these things spake Jesus unto the multitude in parables; and without a parable spake he not unto them:
>
> That it might be fulfilled which was spoken by the prophet, saying, I will open my mouth in parables; I will utter things which have been kept secret from the foundation of the world [Matt. 13:34-35].

"I will utter things which have been kept secret from the foundation of the world"—nail down that statement. Our Lord is giving us a brand-new truth. The things He is revealing now, in parables, have never been revealed like this in the Old Testament.

> Then Jesus sent the multitude away, and went into the house: and his disciples came unto him, saying, Declare unto us the parable of the tares of the field [Matt. 13:36].

Jesus has sent the multitude away and has gathered His disciples about Him. He is going to interpret the parable of the tares to them. We have already gone over it, but let's read it as the Scripture states it.

> He answered and said unto them, He that soweth the good seed is the Son of man;
>
> The field is the world; the good seed are the children of the kingdom; but the tares are the children of the wicked one;
>
> The enemy that sowed them is the devil; the harvest is the end of the world; and the reapers are the angels.
>
> As therefore the tares are gathered and burned in the fire; so shall it be in the end of this world [Matt. 13:37-40].

This is an exact picture of the condition in Christendom in our day. My Lord never missed His predictions. This has been fulfilled as accurately as anything possibly could be.

> **The Son of man shall send forth his angels, and they shall gather out of his kingdom all things that offend, and them which do iniquity [Matt. 13:41].**

You see, in the Kingdom during the Millennium there will be *evil* rearing its ugly head. But it will be taken out.

> **And shall cast them into a furnace of fire: there shall be wailing and gnashing of teeth.**

> **Then shall the righteous shine forth as the sun in the kingdom of their Father. Who hath ears to hear, let him hear [Matt. 13:42–43].**

These harsh words of Scripture came from the gentle lips of our wonderful Lord.

The last three parables are unusual in that they deal with certain different aspects of the Kingdom of Heaven as it is today.

THE PARABLE OF THE TREASURE HID IN A FIELD

> **Again, the kingdom of heaven is like unto treasure hid in a field; the which when a man hath found, he hideth, and for joy thereof goeth and selleth all that he hath, and buyeth that field [Matt. 13:44].**

The "treasure" is Israel. The "field" is the world. The "man" is the Son of man who gave Himself to redeem the nation Israel. This is not a sinner buying the gospel because the gospel is not hidden in a field. Israel, however, is actually buried in the world today. Someone says, "Well, they are a nation right now." They are, but they certainly are having a struggle. They will not be able to enjoy their land until they receive it from the Lord Jesus Christ.

I was very much interested in reading a paper that came from Israel concerning a convention of certain scientists. In a picture I noted above the platform a great sign, printed in both Hebrew and English, which read something like this SCIENCE WILL BRING PEACE TO THIS LAND. May I say to you, friend, science will not bring peace to Israel—nor to any country. Only the Prince of Peace is able to do that.

Actually, Israel is buried throughout the world. The largest population of Jews is not in Israel but is in New York City. And Jewish people are scattered throughout the world. But God is not through with Israel as a nation. The apostle Paul wrote: "I say then, Hath God cast away his people? God forbid. For I also am an Israelite, of the seed of Abraham, of the tribe of Benjamin. God hath not cast away his people which he foreknew . . ." (Rom. 11:1–2).

Paul believed that the Lord was not through with Israel. Zechariah, one of the last writers in the Old Testament, wrote that a new day would come for Israel: "And I will pour upon the house of David, and upon the inhabitants of Jerusalem, the spirit of grace and of supplications: and they shall look upon me whom they have pierced, and they shall mourn for him, as one mourneth for his only son, and shall be in bitterness for him, as one that is in bitterness for his firstborn" (Zech. 12:10).

The prophet Jeremiah in many passages speaks of the regathering of the people of Israel and of God bringing them to their own land. That time is still future. When God regathers them, it will be by miracles so great that they will even forget their miraculous deliverance from Egypt which has been celebrated longer than any other religious holiday. God is not through with the nation Israel, and this parable makes that fact very clear. Israel is the treasure hid in a field, and Christ is the One who "for joy thereof goeth and selleth all that he hath, and buyeth that field." In fact, He gave *Himself* to redeem the nation. Our Lord purchased them with His blood, just as He bought your salvation and my salvation. Zechariah writes of the cleansing which will take place at the time of Christ's return to this earth: "In that day there shall be a fountain opened to the house of David and to the inhabitants of Jerusalem for sin and for uncleanness" (Zech. 13:1).

THE PARABLE OF THE PEARL OF GREAT PRICE

Again, the kingdom of heaven is like unto a merchant man, seeking goodly pearls:

Who, when he had found one pearl of great price, went and sold all that he had, and bought it [Matt. 13:45–46].

The popular interpretation of this parable says that the sinner is the merchantman and the pearl of great price is Christ. The sinner sells all that he has that he might buy Christ. One hymn says:

> I have found the pearl of greatest price.
> My heart doth sing for joy.
> And sing I must for Christ is mine;
> Christ shall my song employ.

I cannot accept this interpretation, and I have dismissed it as unworthy of thoughtful consideration. To begin with, *who* is looking for goodly pearls? Are sinners looking for salvation? My Bible does not read that way, nor has that been my experience as a minister. Sinners are not looking for salvation. The merchantman cannot be the sinner because he has nothing with which to pay. To begin with, he is not seeking Christ, and if he were, how could he buy Him? The merchantman sells all that he has—how can a sinner sell all that he has when he is *dead* in trespasses and sins (see Eph. 2:1)? Further, the Scriptures are very clear that Christ and salvation are not for sale. Salvation is a gift—"For God so loved the world, that he gave his only begotten Son, that whosoever believeth in him should not perish, but have everlasting life" (John 3:16). God so loved that He *gave*. And in Romans 6:23 we are told that "the *gift* of God is eternal life through Jesus Christ our Lord."

The correct interpretation of this parable reveals Christ as the merchantman. He left His heavenly home and came to this earth to find a pearl of great price. He found lost sinners and died for them by shedding His precious blood. He sold all that He had to buy us and redeem us to God. Paul told this to the Corinthians: "For ye know the grace of our Lord Jesus Christ, that, though he was rich, yet for your sakes he became poor, that ye through his poverty might be rich" (2 Cor. 8:9). He redeems us to God—He bought us.

Now let's look at the pearl for a moment. The pearl represents the church. A pearl is not a stone like the diamond. It is formed by a living organism. A grain of sand or other foreign matter intrudes itself into the shell of a small sea creature. It hurts and harms it. The response of the organism is to send out a secretion that coats over the foreign matter. That fluid builds up until a pearl is formed—not a ruby or a diamond, but a beautiful white pearl. A pearl is not like other gems. It cannot be cut to enhance its beauty. It is formed intact. The minute you cut it, you ruin it.

The pearl was never considered very valuable by the Israelites. Several verses of Scripture give us this impression. For example, in Job 28:18 pearls are classed with coral. Although the pearl was not considered valuable among the Hebrews, it was very valuable to the Gentiles. When Christ used the figure of "goodly pearls" (v. 45), I imagine that His disciples wondered why. Oriental people gave to the pearl a symbolic meaning of innocence and purity, fit only for kings and potentates.

With this information in our thinking, let's look again at the parable.

Christ came to this earth as the merchantman. He saw man in sin, and He took man's sin and bore it in His own body. Our sin was an intrusion upon Him—it was that foreign matter. And He was *made* sin for us. As someone has put it, I got into the heart of Christ by a spear wound. Christ ". . . was wounded for our transgressions, he was bruised for our iniquities . . ." (Isa. 53:5).

Notice Christ's response to the sinner. He puts around us His own righteousness. He covers us with His own white robe of righteousness. ". . . we are his workmanship, created in Christ Jesus . . ." (Eph. 2:10). Christ sees us, not as we are now but as we shall be someday, presented to Him as ". . . a glorious church, not having spot, or wrinkle, or any such thing; but that it should be holy and without blemish" (Eph. 5:27). Christ sold all that He had in order that He might gain the church. "Beloved, now are we the sons of God, and it doth not yet appear what we shall be: but we know that, when he shall appear, we shall be like him; for we shall see him as he is" (1 John 3:2).

When we come to the last book of the Bible, the Book of the Revelation, we find a description of the New Jerusalem, the future home of the church. Notice the emblem on the outside of the city—the gates are made of *pearls!* That is no accident, friend; it is planned that way by Christ's design. He is the merchantman "Who, when he had found one pearl of great price, went and sold all that he had, and bought it."

THE PARABLE OF THE NET CAST INTO THE SEA

Again, the kingdom of heaven is like unto a net, that was cast into the sea, and gathered of every kind:

Which, when it was full, they drew to shore, and sat down, and gathered the goods into vessels, but cast the bad away.

So shall it be at the end of the world: the angels shall come forth, and sever the wicked from among the just [Matt. 13:47–49].

"So shall it be at the end of the world"—the word *world* is the Greek *aiōn,* meaning "age." The Bible does not teach the end of this world. It is true that time will be no more, but then eternity begins, and as far as I'm concerned, I can't tell the difference (and I have never met anyone else who could). The end of the age simply means the time when Christ will return to establish His Kingdom on earth.

And shall cast them into the furnace of fire: there shall be wailing and gnashing of teeth [Matt. 13:50].

Our Lord makes it clear in this section that it is a terrible thing to be *lost.*

I was very much interested in reading a scientific paper written by men who were presenting certain scientific evidence in several different fields, and their point was that science was not sure of many things. For example, they were not sure exactly what the atom blast would do. They were not sure of the consequences of germ warfare. They were not sure about the effect of the birth control pill. And many other things were mentioned. Then one of the scientists said this, "It's just like this matter of eternity. You may not *know* whether there is a heaven or a hell, but you had better make sure that you are going to heaven because even if you happen to be wrong, you'll be all right. But if you are wrong, it is surely going to be bad." And our Lord made it very clear that it is indeed going to be very bad.

It is considered sophisticated in our day to be a suave person. Certainly, you will not be considered a square if you deny the existence of hell. But, my friend, in reality you don't know a thing about it, do you? You may say, "Well, you don't know either." Well I know what is in this Book. And since the Bible has been accurate in everything it has predicted, and since in my own life I have proven it true, I take it for granted that it is accurate in its description of hell. And I work on that premise—and it's more than a premise.

If you were told that a hurricane was going to hit your town, what would you do? After you had been given the information, someone might come along and say, "Oh, they warned of a hurricane ten years ago, and no hurricane came." I think you would say "Well, they might have been wrong ten years ago, but they could be right this time; so I think I'll go to a storm cellar." You would be a fool if you didn't. What about the man who rejects Christ's warning of hell? He says, "I'll take my chance." It will be too bad if he is wrong. Our Lord Jesus Himself makes this fact very clear in this parable when He says, "the angels shall come forth, and sever the wicked from among the just, and shall cast them into the furnace of fire: there shall be wailing and gnashing of teeth."

THE PARABLE OF THE HOUSEHOLDER

Some of the people call this verse a parable and others do not. Nevertheless, the content of this single verse has an important message for us.

> Then said he unto them, Therefore every scribe which is
> instructed unto the kingdom of heaven is like unto a
> man that is an householder, which bringeth forth out of
> his treasure things new and old [Matt. 13:52].

This is a very personal verse, especially for those of us who teach and
preach the Word of God. I am to bring forth both the old and new.
Some folk say to me, "Oh, I've heard all of that before." Of course they
have. But it is my business to bring forth old things, and I do hope to
bring forth a few new thoughts, also.

JESUS RETURNS TO HIS OWN COUNTRY
AND IS REJECTED

After teaching these parables, the Lord Jesus departed and headed
toward Nazareth, His hometown.

> And when he was come into his own country, he taught
> them in their synagogue, insomuch that they were as-
> tonished, and said, Whence hath this man this wisdom,
> and these mighty works? [Matt. 13:54].

Let me call your attention again to the fact that in Christ's day they
never questioned whether or not He could perform miracles. Their
question was, "Whence hath this man this wisdom, and these mighty
works?" Where does He get His wisdom, and how can He do these
mighty works?

> Is not this the carpenter's son? is not his mother called
> Mary? and his brethren, James, and Joses, and Simon,
> and Judas? [Matt. 13:55].

"Is not this the carpenter's son?" That was what confused them. They
did not recognize who He really was. To them He was just a carpenter's son. And that is all He is to some folk in our day. They think He

was a great teacher, a great man, a wonderful person, but to them He was only a carpenter's son.

> **And his sisters, are they not all with us? Whence then hath this man all these things? [Matt. 13:56].**

It is obvious that the Lord Jesus had brothers and sisters—of course, they were half brothers and half sisters, younger than He was, and born of Mary and Joseph. They did not understand until after His resurrection that He was truly the Son of God.

> **And they were offended in him. But Jesus said unto them, A prophet is not without honour, save in his own country, and in his own house [Matt. 13:57].**

You see, His hometown folk were so familiar with Him and with His family that they were "offended in him." That is, they took offense at Him. I suppose they said, "We know His family. He grew up among us. Where does He get the things He teaches?"

> **And he did not many mighty works there because of their unbelief [Matt. 13:58].**

This is a tremendous revelation. Note what it was that limited the power of God when He was here. It was unbelief! "He did not many mighty works there because of their unbelief." It was not that He was unable to do them; but because of their *unbelief,* He did very few miracles there. My friend, the great problem with you and me is that we do not have faith to believe—and I'm talking about faith for the salvation of men and women. We need the kind of faith that believes Christ can save the lost. He is limited today in your own community, in your church, in your family, and in your own life by *unbelief.* And this is certainly true of me also. Our Lord states a great truth here. Let's not bypass it.

BIBLIOGRAPHY
(Recommended for Further Study)

Frank, Harry Thomas, editor. *Hammond's Atlas of the Bible Lands.* Maplewood, New Jersey: Hammond Inc., 1977. (Excellent and inexpensive.)

Gaebelein, Arno C. *The Gospel of Matthew.* Neptune, New Jersey: Loizeaux Brothers, Inc., 1910.

Ironside, H. A. *Expository Notes on the Gospel of Matthew.* Neptune, New Jersey: Loizeaux Brothers, Inc., n.d. (Especially good for young Christians.)

Kelley, William. *Lectures on the Gospel of Matthew.* Neptune, New Jersey: Loizeaux Brothers, Inc., 1868.

McGee, J. Vernon. *Moving Thru Matthew.* Pasadena, California: Thru the Bible Books, 1955. (An outline study.)

Pentecost, J. Dwight. *The Parables of Our Lord.* Grand Rapids, Michigan: Zondervan Publishing House, 1982.

Pentecost, J. Dwight. *The Words and Works of Jesus Christ.* Grand Rapids, Michigan: Zondervan Publishing House, 1981.

Scroggie, W. Graham. *A Guide to the Gospels.* London: Pickering & Inglis, 1948. (Excellent for personal or group study.)

Thomas, W. H. Griffith. *Outline Studies in Matthew.* Grand Rapids, Michigan: Eerdmans, 1961.

Toussaint, Stanley D. *Matthew: Behold the King.* Portland, Oregon: Multnomah Press, 1980.

Vos, Howard F. *Beginnings in the Life of Christ.* Chicago, Illinois: Moody Press, 1975.

Vos, Howard F. *Matthew: A Study Guide Commentary*. Grand Rapids, Michigan: Zondervan Publishing House, 1979.

Walvoord, John F. *Gospel of Matthew*. Chicago, Illinois: Moody Press, 1975.